TEN THINGS
SATAN DOESN'T WANT YOU TO KNOW

10

THINGS SATAN
DOESN'T WANT YOU
TO KNOW

Ten Christian Leaders Share Their Insights

Multnomah Publishers *Sisters, Oregon*

TEN THINGS SATAN DOESN'T WANT YOU TO KNOW
published by Multnomah Publishers, Inc.

© 1998 by Multnomah Publishers, Inc.
International Standard Book Number: 1-57673-303-3

Scripture quotations are from:
New American Standard Bible (NASB) © 1960, 1977 by the Lockman Foundation

The Holy Bible, New International Version (NIV) © 1973, 1984 by International Bible Society,
used by permission of Zondervan Publishing House

The Holy Bible, New King James Version (NKJV) © 1984 by Thomas Nelson, Inc.

The Holy Bible King James Version (KJV)

Revised Standard Version Bible (RSV) © 1946, 1952 by the Division of Christian Education
of the National Council of the Churches of Christ in the United States of America

The publishers have generously granted permission to use extended quotations from copyrighted
works. These are cited on page 199.

Multnomah is a registered trademark of Multnomah Publishers, Inc.
The colophon is a trademark of Multnomah Publishers, Inc.

Printed in the United States of America

For information:
MULTNOMAH PUBLISHERS, INC.•POST OFFICE BOX 1720•SISTERS, OREGON 97759

Library of Congress Cataloging-in-Publication Data:
10 things Satan doesn't want you to know / [compiled by] John Van Diest.
    p. cm.
Contents: The good side of the bad news/Charles R. Swindoll—Sowing perversion, deception, and dis-
cord/Billy Graham—Who won the showdown in the desert?/Ron Mehl—The battle between the
Kingdoms/Charles W. Colson—The serpent is doomed/Erwin W. Lutzer—How Satan causes you to
sin/John Piper—Don't listen to your loins/Jay Carty—New Age or old lie?/Kerry D. McRoberts—Win-
ning over Satan's shenanigans/Charles C. Ryrie—The awesome power of prayer/Ray C. Stedman.
    ISBN 1-57673-303-3 (alk. paper)
    1. Devil. 2. Spiritual life—Christianity. I. Van Diest, John.
    BT981.A18   1998   98-17018
    235'.47—dc21   CIP

98 99 00 01 02 03 04 05 — 10 9 8 7 6 5 4 3 2 1

CONTENTS

INTRODUCTION

Of all the mistakes we make, it is quite possible that underestimating Satan's ability to lure us away from truth tops the list! Like a magician with his "bag of tricks" his illusions have swayed many people. His ability to make bad look good, ugly look beautiful, absolute look relative, and lust look like love are just a few of his scams.

Satan was initially created as a great angel called a cherub. He wanted to be like God and that's when the trouble began. As a "fallen" angel he has been on a collision course with God ever since. He now masquerades as an "angel of light," opposing good and promoting evil.

Satan loves to keep us ignorant about God, about Christ, about the Bible, and about his own existence. In fact, ignorance may be his greatest tool.

This book is designed to expose the truth about Satan and his tactics. I've chosen ten major things he doesn't want us to know, and I've included the good news: we can be victorious over him!

Be aware.

John Van Diest
GENERAL EDITOR

THE GOOD SIDE OF
THE BAD NEWS

CHARLES R. SWINDOLL

Charles R. Swindoll, D. D.
President, Dallas Theological Seminary
President, Insight for Living radio ministry
Author of nine Gold Medallion books

I like good news. Therefore, I prefer to emphasize the happy, bright, colorful side of life. But my problem with that emphasis is this: That is only *half* the message of Christianity. When we stop to think about it, we really cannot appreciate the bright and beautiful side of life until we know how dark and dismal the backdrop is. So, to be true to my calling and to be complete in the presentation of biblical doctrine, it is necessary to expose, along with the bright side of life, the dark side.

It was back in 1886 that Robert Louis Stevenson wrote a classic story that exposed everybody's life. He called it *Dr. Jekyll and Mr. Hyde.* Although a little older, Stevenson was a contemporary of Mark Twain, the American storyteller. And perhaps it was from that story that Twain came up with the statement so familiar to all of us: "Everybody is a moon; and has a dark side which he never shows to anybody."[1]

No one ever said it better than Jesus when He spoke so sternly against the hypocrisy of the Pharisees and scribes.

"Woe to you, scribes and Pharisees, hypocrites! For you are like whitewashed tombs which on the outside appear beautiful, but inside they are full of dead men's bones and all uncleanness. Even so you too outwardly appear righteous to men, but inwardly you are full of hypocrisy and lawlessness." (Matthew 23:27–28)

Lest you live under the delusion that the "dark side" was a problem only former generations struggled with, just think about your life over the past several days. Think inwardly rather than outwardly. More than likely you behaved yourself rather well externally…but not from within! Call to mind the impulses, the drives, the secrets, the motives behind the actions you lived out. Perhaps a few of them did surface, but most of your dark side remained hidden to the public. French essayist Michael de Montaigne put it this way:

There is a man so good, who, were he to submit all his thoughts and actions to the laws, would not deserve hanging ten times in his life.[2]

DEPRAVITY DEFINED AND EXPLAINED

My opening statements in this chapter have to do with our most ancient and all-pervasive disease. It's helpful to remember that the deadliest killer of humanity is not heart disease or cancer…it is depravity. Every one of us has it. Every one of us suffers from the consequences of it. And to make matters even worse, we pass it on to each new generation. It has spread to all men.

One of the most sweeping, broad-brush statements in all of Scripture on the depravity of humanity is found in Genesis 6:5:

> Then the LORD saw that the wickedness of man was great on the earth, and that every intent of the thoughts of his heart was only evil continually.

Are you as gripped as I am when I read three words in that verse? Look at them again: "every," "only," "continually." The scene described in this verse is an inescapable, universal cesspool in the inner person of all humanity—a hidden source of pollution that lies at the root of wrong. Even from childhood this is true.

A number of years ago the Minnesota Crime Commission released this statement:

> Every baby starts life as a little savage. He is completely selfish and self-centered. He wants what he wants when he wants it—his bottle, his mother's attention, his play-mates' toy, his uncle's watch. Deny him these once, and he seethes with rage and aggressiveness, which would be murderous were he not so helpless. He is, in fact, dirty. He has no morals, no knowledge, no skills. This means that all children—not just certain children—are born delinquent. If permitted to continue in the self-centered world of his infancy, given free reign to his impulsive actions to satisfy his wants, every child would grow up a criminal—a thief, a killer, or a rapist.

Now that's reality. And if it's your tendency as a positive thinker to ignore it, it still won't go away. If it's your tendency as a parent to ignore it, that root of depravity will come back to haunt you in your home. A permissive, think-only-about-the-bright-side-of-life philosophy will be eaten alive by problems of depravity as your child grows up without restraints and without controls. Not even a kind and professional Dr. Jekyll could remove the savagelike Mr. Hyde from his own life. Face it, the dark side is here to stay.

Psalm 51 is another section of Scripture worth examining as we come to terms with depravity. It is the psalm David wrote following Nathan's confrontation with him after the adultery-murder-hypocrisy scandal.

> Be gracious to me, O God, according to Thy lovingkind-ness; according to the greatness of Thy compassion blot out my transgressions. Wash me thoroughly from my iniquity, and cleanse me from my sin. For I know my transgressions, and my sin is ever before me. Against Thee, Thee only, I have sinned, and done what is evil in Thy sight, so that Thou art justified when Thou dost speak, and blameless when Thou dost judge. Behold, I was brought forth in iniquity, and in sin my mother conceived me. (Psalm 51:1–5)

He begins with a plea for grace, which shouldn't surprise us. The only way David could expect to survive would be by the grace of God. That's the reason *any* of us survive! What is grace? How would you define it? Probably, the most popular two-word definition is "unmerited favor." To amplify that a bit: grace is what God does for mankind, which we do not deserve, which we cannot earn, and which we will never be able to repay. Awash in our sinfulness, helpless to change on our own, polluted to the core which no possibility of cleaning ourselves up we cry out for grace. It is our only hope.

That's why David's prayer begins, "Be gracious." He doesn't deserve God's favor. He's fallen into sin. His life is a mess. So he asks that God would be gracious according to His lovingkindness.

Following his unguarded, open confession, David addresses the nucleus of his problem. He was "brought forth in iniquity" because his mother conceived him "in sin." He doesn't mean that the act of conception was sinful. The *Amplified Bible* handles the meaning quite well:

> Behold, I was brought forth in [a state of iniquity; my mother was sinful who conceived me [and I, too, am sinful].

I have come from sinful parents, and therefore I have had the same disease passed on to me...so please be gracious to me, O God. That's the idea.

Lest we feel a little smug, thinking that David was all alone in the struggle against sin, let's return to the Jekyll-and-Hyde reminder...we've *all* got the disease. Depravity affects all of us. Because Adam fell, we, too, fell. Theologian Dwight Pentecost addresses the issue of Adam's fall. Read his words carefully:

> One of the most important questions which you can face is the question, "How far did Adam fall?" A number of different answers have been given to that question.
>
> The liberal says that Adam fell upward, so that

Adam's lot was better after the fall than before the fall because something was added to the personality of Adam of which he had been deprived previously. Consequently, Adam was a fuller and more complete person after the fall than he was before the fall. There are those who say that when Adam fell, he fell over the cliff, but that when he was going over the cliff he grabbed something on the top of the cliff and held on. He fell downward, but he held on before he slipped over the brink, and if he exerts enough will and enough strength he can pull himself back up over the brink and stand on solid ground again. Those who have that concept are trying to lift themselves by their own bootstraps and work their way into heaven.

Then, there is the teaching that says that when Adam fell, he slipped over the brink but he landed on a ledge part way down and that the ledge is the church and the church will lift him up and put him on solid ground again.

But the Word of God says that when Adam fell he fell all the way. He became depraved, totally depraved, unable to do anything to please God. He is under sin, dead, under judgment, under Satan's control; he is lost.[3]

HUMANITY SURVEYED AND EXPOSED

One of the wonderful things about the Bible, which only adds to its credibility, is that it tells us the truth, the whole truth, and nothing but the truth regarding its characters. I often say it doesn't airbrush the portraits. When it paints its heroes, it paints them warts and all. The scars are not hidden. And about the time you're tempted to elevate certain men and women in Scripture to a pedestal of worship, God brings them down to size. Each one is completely, totally, and thoroughly H-U-M-A-N. They are all as James refers to Elijah: "a man with a nature like ours" (James 5:17).

THREE OLD TESTAMENT CHARACTERS

Noah

I'd like to introduce the first man, who appears in Genesis, chapter 6. What a wonderful man he was! We need to be reminded of the times in which he lived. We just read about that awful scene in Genesis 6:5 as it described Noah's surroundings. The Lord said that he was grieved that He had even made man. And so before judging humanity with the flood, He surveyed the world, looking for one who would qualify as a righteous man. And He found one, only one, who found favor in His sight. His name was Noah.

These are the records of the generations of Noah. Noah was a righteous man, blameless in his time; Noah walked with God. (Genesis 6:9)

This verse says three things about Noah: He was righteous, blameless, and he walked with God. That's quite a resume! Here is a good man, surrounded by gross wickedness...a flower growing out of a cesspool. He was so good, God appointed him to build the ark and to save his family from death. And that's exactly what Noah did. He worked on it consistently for 120 years. And while he worked, he preached. And as he preached, he warned. And when he finished the ark, he got his family inside, though nobody else was interested, and the flood came. They alone were saved from destruction. It's one of those stories we never tire of hearing. And Noah comes out, of course, smelling like a rose. Public hero number one!

Chapter 9 brings us to the end of the flood and presents Noah and his family to a new earth.

Here stands a man who has been walking with God for all these years. What a model of courage and determination! But as soon as we're about to fall on our knees to worship him...we find he has feet of clay. Yes, even Noah. Unlike the moon, he is forced to show his dark side.

> Then Noah began farming and planted a vineyard. And he drank of the wine and became drunk, and uncovered himself inside his tent. And Ham, the father of Canaan, saw the nakedness of his father, and told his two brothers outside. (Genesis 9:20–22)

I don't pretend to know all that his uncovering himself implies. It was, no doubt, sexually perverse, because his sons were ashamed to be in his presence in his naked condition. On top of that, the man was drunk.

It seems amazing that a good man—so good he was picked above all other men—would get himself drunk in his tent and blatantly uncover himself. So wicked was Noah's disobedience that his sons were not only shamed by it, but cursed because of it. As in the case of Adam and Eve, a divine curse followed disobedience...it is like an instant replay. It's shocking if you forget that even in Noah there was a depraved nature.

Every now and then a once-great man or godly woman will fall. So great will be the fall that their defection will make headline attention in Christian and secular publications alike. Even though we know the doctrine of depravity, we're still stunned.

In one sense it is only natural to be surprised since we trusted the person to live obediently. In another sense we really have no reason to be shocked. Depravity affects us all—and even the so-called heroes of our life occasionally drop through the cracks. Before you become too disillusioned, remember Noah. Not even he was immune. Sometimes there is drunkenness, and sometimes there is sexual perversity. And when the truth comes out, our heroes die a painful death in our minds.

Learn a major lesson from this study: *No one on earth deserves your worship.* You tread on very thin ice when you enshrine any human individual—no matter how mightily he or she is being used of God.

Is it okay to have heroes? Sure it is. And it is certainly appropriate to respect them. But our respect should never come anywhere close to man-worship. When it does, and then your hero suddenly shows his weakness, you are going to be terribly disillusioned. It may not be as scandalous as it was with Noah, but they will fall in some way. They will show intemperance, or anger, or impatience, or even a lack of courtesy. If you get to know them well enough, you'll discover they're just people who have to put their britches on one leg at a time. Just like everyone else.

Try to remember that every person on earth is still a depraved human being. Some are being used by God, but in no way are they free from the disease. Example: Noah…a good man who distinguished himself in bad times…but was still imperfect.

Moses

The second man worth our consideration appears first on the pages of Scripture in Exodus, chapter 2. His name is Moses. I like

Moses. So do you. Who wouldn't like Moses? He comes from an extremely humble origin. He very graciously handles his early successes. Hebrews 11 says that he refused to be called the son of Pharaoh's daughter. And finally, though he was well educated, mighty in words and deeds, and considered by many to be the Pharaoh-elect, he was a man who decided to serve the Lord, rather than himself. And after a lengthy period of preparation he was used to lead the people through the wilderness. You probably know his story.

No other man in Scripture talked with God face to face. When Moses came down from the mountain, his face literally glowed with the Shekinah glory of Jehovah, having been in the presence of God. He was there when the finger of God drilled the Torah into stone. He came down from the mountain and presented the first copies of the written Word of God to the people of God. He oversaw the building of the tabernacle. He led a whole nation through the trackless deserts of the Sinai. He stayed faithfully by their side, though they often came at him with verbal guns blazing.

Now you'd think the man could virtually walk on water, but he couldn't. This same man, Moses, had a record of murder in his life. It occurred during his midlife years.

> Now it came about in those days, when Moses had grown up, that he went out to his brethren and looked on their hard labors; and he saw an Egyptian beating a Hebrew, one of his brethren. So he looked this way and that, and when he saw there was no one around, he struck down the Egyptian and hid him in the sand. (Exodus 2:11–12)

Is that amazing? Well, not really...not if you believe in the depravity of humanity. In an unguarded moment, a moment of rash decision, Moses acted in the flesh as he killed an Egyptian. Yes, in a rage of anger he murdered him. And then tried to hide the evidence. Why? Because he knew he had done wrong.

Forty years later (aged eighty) he's out in the wilderness. He thinks he's going to be leading sheep for the rest of his life. And God steps on the scene and says, "You're the one I have chosen to lead My people out of Egypt." Now here is an eighty-year-old man with murder on his record. He knows that he has failed the Lord, and yet he hears God graciously coming back saying, "You are going to be My spokesman." You would think he would have learned enough to say right away, "Wherever You lead me, I will go." Does he do that? No.

Don't call Moses' response (recorded in Exodus 3:11–4:17) *humility.* It's stubbornness. It's willful resistance.

Moses also battled with a temper—a short fuse. It may have gotten a little longer the older he got, but he never fully conquered it. But those of us who are impatient can't afford to be too critical of Moses. We know what it is to fight a bad temper. We try many ways to keep the fuse wet. When it gets dry it tends to make everything explode. Moses is a man who had that problem. Why? Because he was depraved. He was a good man. He was a leader. He was God's spokesman. But He still had a depraved nature. A Mr. Hyde nature lived inside his Dr. Jekyll skin. You see him on display in these lines from Numbers 20:

And there was no water for the congregation; and they assembled themselves against Moses and Aaron. The people thus contended with Moses and spoke, saying, "If only we had perished when our brothers perished before the LORD! Why then have you brought the LORD's assembly into this wilderness, for us and our beasts to die here? And why have you made us come up from Egypt, to bring us in to this wretched place? It is not a place of grain or figs or vines or pomegranates, nor is there water to drink." Then Moses and Aaron came in from the presence of the assembly to the doorway of the tent of meeting, and fell on their faces. Then the glory of the LORD appeared to them; and the LORD spoke to Moses, saying, "Take the rod; and you and your brother Aaron assemble the congregation and speak to the rock before their eyes, that it may yield its water. You shall thus bring forth water for them out of the rock and let the congregation and their beasts drink." So Moses took the rod from before the LORD, just as He had commanded him; and Moses and Aaron gathered the assembly before the rock. And he said to them, "Listen now, you rebels; shall we bring forth water for you out of this rock?" Then Moses lifted up his hand and struck the rock twice with his rod; and water came forth abundantly, and the congregation and their beasts drank. But the LORD said to Moses and Aaron, "Because you have not believed Me, to treat Me as holy in the sight of the sons of Israel, therefore you shall not bring this assembly into the land which I have given them." (Numbers 20:2–12)

What a story! Many people see only judgment here. I see grace. Did you catch those words? "And water came forth abundantly." If you had been God, would you have brought water out of the rock? No way. But grace brings water even when there's disobedience. Why would Moses, this good man, strike the rock, when God has just said, "Speak to it"? I'm going to repeat it until it sinks in: *Because he was depraved.* Color Moses Blue. He had a dark side he didn't want anybody to see. But on this occasion it was on display.

Before you get too pious and judgmental with Moses, just think about the rods and rocks in your life. Call to mind a few of the times you knew what was best and you did what was worst...when you realized in your heart that patience pays off, yet you acted impatiently. Want to know why you did it? Because *you're* depraved. Because you too have a dark side. Maybe it's a temper. Maybe it's greed. Or gossip. Or lust. Or overeating or drugs and booze. It could be envy, jealousy, or a dozen other things I could name. We all have them and they are often our besetting sins. Depravity reveals itself in numerous ways...all of them dark.

David

Having looked at Noah and Moses, let's consider perhaps the most popular character in the Old Testament, the man after God's heart, King David. My favorite piece of sculpture is a work by Michelangelo, the statue of David—white marble, standing at the end of a long corridor in Florence, Italy. As you study the statue, you stand in awe, not only of an artist's ability with a mallet and chisel but of God's marvelous plan in taking a teenager from a flock of sheep owned by his father and bringing him to lead His people. A beautiful summary of his story appears in Psalm 78.

> He also chose David His servant, and took him from the sheepfolds; from the care of the ewes with suckling lambs

He brought him, to shepherd Jacob His people, and Israel His inheritance. So he shepherded them according to the integrity of his heart, and guided them with his skillful hands. (Psalm 78:70–72)

But the earliest reference to David is found in 1 Samuel 13 as Samuel speaks to Saul—who has forfeited the right to rule the people.

And Samuel said to Saul, "You have acted foolishly; you have not kept the commandment of the LORD your God, which He commanded you, for now the LORD would have established your kingdom over Israel forever. But now your kingdom shall not endure. The LORD has sought out for Himself *a man after His own heart.* (1 Samuel 13:13–14a, emphasis mine)

You could write in the margin of your Bible, "Reference to David." A man after the very heart of God. And David stays faithful to God for well over a dozen years while jealous Saul hunts him down.

Finally, David is given the throne of Israel. He takes a nation that's bottomed-out spiritually, militarily, and economically. He expands its boundaries from 6,000 to 60,000 square miles. He establishes trade routes with the world. He equips them with a respectable military fighting force. David literally puts the nation on the map. He gives Israel a flag that flies higher than it had ever flown before. What a leader. What a hero. What a man of battle. What a courageous, faithful man of God..."a man after His own heart."

If you're looking for somebody to respect as a leader in biblical days, you don't have to go much further than David. David proves himself to be a man who continues to walk with God as he leads the nation correctly and courageously.

Until you get to 2 Samuel, chapter 11.

Until you come to one particular evening.

As king, he should have been in battle with his troops. Instead he was at ease in the palace. And that was how he happened to take a fateful walk on his roof.

> Now when evening came David arose from his bed and walked around on the roof of the king's house, and from the roof he saw a woman bathing; and the woman was very beautiful in appearance. So David sent and inquired about the woman. And one said, "Is this not Bathsheba, the daughter of Eliam, the wife of Uriah the Hittite?" And David sent messengers and took her, and when she came to him, he lay with her; and when she had purified herself from her uncleanness, she returned to her house. And the woman conceived; and she sent and told David, and said, "I am pregnant." (2 Samuel 11:2–5)

You know the rest of the tragic story. Not only had our hero been involved with another woman outside wedlock (he certainly didn't need another woman), he had now found himself in a place of intense compromise and pressure. The thought of abortion was never in their mind—certainly not. But she was pregnant with his child. In a state of panic, David realized he had to do something about her husband Uriah. He tried to mask the story. Brought the man back from battle. Hoped that he would sleep with his wife.

But Uriah, more faithful to the cause of Israel than David was, refused. And finally, the king instructed Joab to put Uriah into the heat of the battle. When that happened, of course, Uriah was killed. Joab sent a messenger back, knowing the heart of his leader, and among other things, he said "You be sure and tell King David that Uriah was killed." The deceptive plot thickened.

I ask you, how could a man as godly as David fall as far as he did with Bathsheba? How could he be responsible for murdering a man on the battlefield? How could he live the life of a hypocrite for almost a year? How could David do that? He's our hero! He's that faithful shepherd! He's the giant killer!

The answer is going to sound terribly familiar—he is depraved. He has a nature that will never improve. He has lust, just like every man and every woman reading these words right now. And he yielded to it. As lust played its sweet song, the king of Israel danced to the music. He was responsible, just as you and I are every time we yield. Like Noah and Moses, David's lapse into sin left him vulnerable to its consequences. When depravity wins a victory, many get hurt...not just the one who is most responsible. Never forget that!

Most of us have been down the pike far enough to know that we cannot trust our sinful nature. Heed this word of counsel: *Don't get yourself in a situation where your nature takes charge.* If you are weakened by lust when you are with the opposite sex, you have to keep yourself out of those tempting situations where you will yield. If you play around the fire, it is only a matter of time. It won't be "if" but "when." And make no mistake about it, it will be your fault because you played the fool. And I can assure you, others will be burned in the same fire.

It is terribly important, especially in the area of personal

morality, that we keep a safe distance when there is the temptation to be involved in illicit activity. I hope you never forget this
warning. We are living in a day when moral purity and marital
infidelity are being rationalized and compromised. More and
more people—more and more *Christians*—are convincing themselves it's okay to fudge a little.

If you're sleeping with somebody who is not your mate, you're
in sin. You're displeasing God. If you're walking away from God in
an area of sexual activity, it is hurting your testimony and hurting
the ministry of Jesus Christ. Face the music and get back in step!
Claim the grace that's coming to you through Christ. Say, as David
finally said "I have sinned," and turn around. Do it now!

And may I add? If you are in ministry and doing that, clean up
your life or get out of the ministry. Do everyone else in ministry a
favor, if you refuse to repent…just step out of the ministry and say,
"I have sinned. I have forfeited the right to lead a flock. I've compromised. I've ruined my personal testimony, but I refuse to ruin the
testimony of the Church." Better still, return to the Lord and claim
His forgiveness. Christ is coming back for His Bride, the Church,
expecting her to be pure, "having no spot or wrinkle or any such
thing; but that she should be holy and blameless" (Ephesians 5:27).

Two New Testament Characters

Before we wrap up this chapter, let's glance at a couple of New
Testament heroes.

Peter

One of those heroes must surely be Peter! Remember his greatest
moment with his fellow disciples and his Lord?

> Now when Jesus came into the district of Caesarea
> Philippi, He began asking His disciples, saying, "Who do
> people say that the Son of Man is?" And they said, "Some
> say John the Baptist; and others, Elijah; but still others,
> Jeremiah, or one of the prophets." He said to them, "But
> who do you say that I am?" And Simon Peter answered
> and said, "Thou are the Christ, the Son of the living God."
> (Matthew 16:13–16)

What a grand statement of faith! Good for you, Peter! With
godliness and uncompromising assurance, the man spoke the
truth. His theology? Impeccable. His faith? Impressive. I think
Jesus wanted to applaud him. He did, in effect, when He told him
that flesh and blood hadn't revealed that to him. Peter's answer
came from the very portals of heaven. "God revealed that to you,
Peter." It was his moment.

A little later on, Peter is again with his Lord. And the Lord is
telling him about the future.

> And Jesus said to them, "You will all fall away, because it
> is written, 'I will strike down the shepherd, and the sheep
> shall be scattered.' But after I have been raised, I will go
> before you to Galilee." But Peter said to Him, "Even
> though all may fall away, yet I will not." (Mark 14:27–29)

Now Peter meant well. I've said things like that, haven't you?
In a moment of great emotional gush, Peter made sweeping
promises to his Lord. Reminds me of the standard New Year's resolution:

Journal Entry: January 1—I'll meet with you every day of
this new year, Lord.
January 4—Lord, I've missed the last two days, but I'm
back.

Let's not be too critical of Peter. The man meant it with all his
heart.

"Even though all may fall away, yet I will not." And Jesus
said to him, "Truly I say to you, that you yourself this very
night, before a cock crows twice, shall three times deny
Me." (Mark 14:29–30)

And that's exactly what happened. The fact is, he later denied
his Lord, openly and unashamedly. How can it be that this sincere
disciple who made such a right-on statement of faith could drift
so far, so fast?

In the same chapter of Mark's Gospel, we find the same man
masking his identity:

He [Peter] began to curse and swear, "I do not know this
man [Jesus] you are talking about!" (Mark 14:71)

Peter's "Mr. Hyde" was on display. A darkness so horrible we
don't even want to imagine it. Peter, however, could never forget it.
And then we read:

And immediately a cock crowed a second time. And
Peter remembered how Jesus had made the remark to

him, "Before a cock crows twice, you will deny Me three times." And he began to weep. (Mark 14:72)

I don't think there is any weeping as bitter as the weeping brought on by spiritual failure. It's downright terrible! I'm thinking of a minister friend of mine who has failed the Lord through sexual compromise. He has stepped away from leadership and ministry. His flock is still in shock. At this very moment he is going through the time of weeping, like Peter. He knows he has forfeited the right to lead. And now that he has repented and come clean, he realizes the heinous condition of his soul during that period of time when he was compromising. I met with him to encourage him. Several times he broke into audible sobs. Like Peter, he was weeping in anguish before God. He is now seeking God's will for his future.

Why did Peter do that? Why did my friend to that? I repeat, at the risk of sounding like a broken record, you and I are prone to wander, prone to leave the God we love *because of the depravity of humanity.*

Paul

Can it be that a man as fine as Paul would be included? Romans, chapter 7, I think, is the finest explanation of humanity's depraved nature found anywhere in the Scriptures. We've looked at Noah and Moses and David. In the New Testament we're looking at Peter and Paul. If I had time, I could also include Mary—Peter, Paul, and Mary (couldn't resist it). But we'll stop with Paul.

Listen to the personal testimony of a great man of God, the theologian par excellence, the missionary, the apostle, the founder of churches, the man who forged out the finer points of our theology, who wrote more of the New Testament than any other writer. Read Paul's admission slowly and thoughtfully:

> I do not understand what I do. For what I want to do I do not do, but what I hate I do. And if I do what I do not want to do, I agree that the law is good. As it is, it is no longer I myself who do it, but it is sin living in me. I know that nothing good lives in me, that is, in my sinful nature. For I have the desire to do what is good, but I cannot carry it out. For what I do is not the good I want to do; no, the evil I do not want to do—this I keep on doing. Now if I do what I do not want to do, it is no longer I who do it, but it is sin living in me that does it.
>
> So I find this law at work: When I want to do good, evil is right there with me. For in my inner being I delight in God's law; but I see another law at work in the members of my body, waging war against the law of my mind and making me a prisoner of the law of sin at work within my members. What a wretched man I am! Who will rescue me from this body of death? (Romans 7:15–24, NIV)

I hardly need to amplify. Paul's testimony is everyone's testimony. That's why we sin. That's why the ark builder got drunk and why a leader lost his temper and why a king committed adultery and why a disciple denied his Lord. Even though we wish to do good, evil is present in us...all of us. John R. W. Stott said it best:

> We human beings have both a unique dignity as creatures made in God's image and a unique depravity as sinners under his judgment. The former gives us hope;

the latter places a limit on our expectations. Our Christian critique of the secular mind is that it tends to be either too naively optimistic or too negatively pessimistic in its estimates of the human condition, whereas the Christian mind, firmly rooted in biblical realism, both celebrates the glory and deplores the shame of our human being. We can behave like God in whose image we are made, only to descend to the level of the beasts. We are able to think, choose, create, love, and worship, but also to refuse to think, to choose evil, to destroy, to hate, and to worship ourselves. We build churches and drop bombs. We develop intensive care units for the critically ill and use the same technology to torture political enemies who presume to disagree with us. This is "man," a strange bewildering paradox, dust of earth and breath of God, shame and glory.[4]

THE ONE GREAT EXCEPTION

Jesus Christ is the exception—no shame in Him, only glory. No dark side, only light. No blue, only spotless white.

The Scripture says three things of Christ. He *knew* no sin; He *had* no sin; He *did* no sin. No sin nature. Born without sin. Lived without sinfulness. Knowing no sin, having no sin, doing no sin, He qualified as the Lamb of God who took away the power of sin and the dread of death. Therefore, when we confess our sins, He hears us and cleanses us. What a relief! We confess "Guilty as charged." He answers, "Heard and forgiven!"

And this is the message we have heard from Him and announce to you, that God is light, and in Him there is no darkness at all. If we say that we have fellowship with Him and yet walk in the darkness, we lie and do not practice the truth; but if we walk in the light as He Himself is in the light, we have fellowship with one another, and the blood of Jesus His Son cleanses us from all sin. If we say that we have no sin, we are deceiving ourselves, and the truth is not in us. If we confess our sins, He is faithful and righteous to forgive us our sins and to cleanse us from all unrighteousness. (1 John 1:5–9)

TWO OPTIONS—CHOOSE ONE

When we boil the options down to basics, we really have two choices. *First, we can choose to live as victims* of our depravity...for "evil is present in me," as Paul wrote. Or *second, we can choose to live as victors* through the power of Jesus Christ. The last thing I desire to do is to leave in your mind the impression that you must spend your years as a helpless, pitiful victim of depravity.

Each one of these people we've studied made a deliberate decision to sin. They weren't duped. It came as no sudden surprise. They *chose* to live as victims, at least at that moment.

Let me encourage you to live as a victor through the power of Jesus Christ. Start by coming to the cross, by faith. Ask Christ to come into your life. Then as you face evil, as you come across it, as it rears its head in temptation, claim the power of God that Christ offers, now that He's living within you.

You can say, "Lord, right now, at this moment, I am weak. You're strong. By Your strength I'm stepping away from evil, and Your power is going to give me the grace to get through it victoriously. Take charge right now." And walk away. Stand firm!

Remember the old gospel song "Just As I Am"? It is used at

the close of every Billy Graham Crusade. While attending the crusade at Anaheim Stadium in 1985, I listened to that song night after night as thousands of people poured onto the playing field to turn their lives over to Jesus Christ. Some were lost; some were saved. But all sought help with the same problem—their sin. Only the Lamb of God can solve that problem.

> Just as I am, without one plea,
> But that Thy blood was shed for me,
> And that Thou bidd'st me come to Thee,
> O Lamb of God, I come! I come!
>
> Just as I am and waiting not
> To rid my soul of one dark blot,
> To Thee whose blood can cleanse each spot.
> O Lamb of God, I come! I come!
>
> Just as I am. Thou wilt receive,
> Wilt welcome, pardon, cleanse, receive,
> Because Thy promise I believe,
> O Lamb of God, I come! I come![5]

Mr. Hyde has a greater bark than a bite. Trust me...no, trust God's Word. The Lord Jesus will help you face reality. He will see you through. Come to the Lamb of God. Hear again His promise of forgiveness.

> Forgive us, Lord...for the things we have done that make us feel uncomfortable in Thy presence. All the front that we polish so carefully for men to see does not deceive Thee. For Thou knowest every thought that has left its

shadow on our memory. Thou hast marked every motive that curdled something sweet within us.

We acknowledge—with bitterness and true repentance—that cross and selfish thoughts have entered our minds; we acknowledge that we have permitted our minds to wander through unclean and forbidden ways; we have toyed with that which we knew was not for us; we have desired that which we should not have.

We acknowledge that often we have deceived ourselves where our plain duty lay.

We confess before Thee that our ears are often deaf to the whisper of Thy call, our eyes often blind to the signs of Thy guidance.

Make us willing to be changed, even though it requires surgery of the soul and the therapy of discipline.

Make our hearts warm and soft, that we may receive now the blessing of Thy forgiveness, the benediction of Thy "Depart in peace…and sin no more." Amen.[6]

—Peter Marshall

SOWING PERVERSION, DECEPTION AND DISCORD

BILLY GRAHAM

Billy Graham, D. D.
World-renowned evangelist
Special advisor to six U.S. presidents
Author of bestselling books

One afternoon in Paris, Ruth answered a knock on our hotel room door. Two men stood there. One explained in broken English that the other was "the Messiah" who had come to see me on a "divine errand." After a brief, pathetic encounter with another of the deranged people who have come my way claiming to be the Messiah, Ruth remarked to me, "He claimed to be Christ, but he couldn't even speak to us in our own language." There is a vast menagerie of masquerading messiahs in the world today—both men and women—claiming to be the Christ. Some of them are mental or emotional cripples. Others scheme and dream with ever more menacing motives and powers. But all of them are counterfeits.

The Bible promises that this line of false christs will grow longer and longer until the final embodiment of antichrist appears at the head of the procession. He will be Satan's man. Imitating

Christ, he offers peace, but he is as false as the peace he offers. His golden age will be short-lived.

Some of the deceivers around us are more obviously in league with Satan and the satanic than others. Some make no overt attempts to deceive; they speak directly of the tempting powers of evil and call men and women to worship at the feet of Satan himself. Overt Satan worship is perhaps the easiest deception to see through.

With nearly a million copies in print today, *The Satanist Bible* declares the aims, purposes, and practices of Satan worshipers. Under the guidance of leaders such as Anton LaVey and Michael Aquino, the Satanists persuade thousands of deluded men, women, and especially teenagers, to follow them in their hellish practices. As the author of books such as *Satanic Rituals* and *The Complete Witch,* LaVey is perhaps the best-known, most persuasive Satanist priest in America.

PERVERSION OF THE GOOD

Jerry Johnston's book, *The Edge of Evil: The Rise of Satanism in North America,* gives a startling portrait of the real dangers of Satanism and other "black arts" in our society. Johnston describes the way young people are recruited, introduced to the bizarre rituals and practices of Satanism, and even included in evil sacrifices. The book shows how innocent "seekers" are systematically led into a life in the occult.

What is the danger in such beliefs? In his classic book, *Those Curious New Cults,* William J. Petersen, former editor of *Eternity* magazine, says, "The most infamous blasphemy of Satanist ritual is the Black Mass" (p. 80). Petersen describes how, in the Black Mass, the participants try to reverse everything they know about Christianity. The crucifix is hung upside down. The alter is covered in black instead of white. Hymns are sung backward. The rite is performed by a defrocked priest, and whenever the Lord or Christ is mentioned, the priest spits on the altar or worse. To make the blasphemy even more despicable, sexual rites are added. Sometimes a child is even slain. During the ceremony, the worshipers renounce their faith, acknowledge Satan as Lord, and, when the ritual concludes, the high priest closes with a curse rather than a blessing.

Regardless of how obviously evil or repulsive all this may seem, you should remember that it is not fiction. It is not even rare any more. There are thousands of Satanists in the world today. In my travels throughout the world I have seen innumerable varieties of Satan worshipers. One night in Nuremberg, Germany, we were holding a crusade in the same stadium in which Hitler used to stage his infamous rallies. It was difficult to sit in that place and hear in the echoes of memory the masses shouting, "Sieg, Heil!" We realized that from this place the Third Reich had marched out to wage war on the world and, in the pursuit of its pagan ideologies, to exterminate millions of Jews and other prisoners held for political, religious, and psychological reasons. But we were reaching sixty thousand people a night in that open arena. They were singing Christ's praises, and I was preaching the Word of God. Thousands were coming to accept Jesus Christ as Savior and Lord. The presence of God's people there seemed to exorcise the old demons that had stalked those aisles so many years before.

Then one night, as I sat on the platform, Satan worshipers dressed in black assembled just outside the stadium doors. Using ancient, evil rites, they tried to put a hex on the meeting. The rumor of their presence spread, Christians prayed, and in answer to those prayers, nothing came of the incident.

THE POWER OF PRAYER

Another night in Chicago, three hundred Satan worshipers approached McCormick Place with the specific intent of taking over the platform and stopping the crusade service that was in progress. They announced their plan in advance, but I didn't dream they would actually try to storm the platform. We had just sung the second hymn of the evening. George Beverly Shea had sung a gospel song, and Cliff Barrows was about to lead a massed choir in a great anthem of praise. At that moment a policeman rushed to the stage and whispered something to the mayor, who was present that night to welcome us.

At the same moment, the Satan worshipers forced their way past the ushers at the rear of that spacious auditorium and were proceeding down the back aisles toward the platform. There were more than thirty thousand young people in our Youth Night service. Only those seated near the back saw the Satan worshipers enter. The mayor of Chicago turned to me and said, "Dr. Graham, we'll let the police handle these intruders."

We never call in the police for crusade duty if we can help it. "Let me try it another way, Mr. Mayor," I suggested. I then interrupted the choir's song and addressed the thirty thousand young people there in McCormick Place. I explained, "There are about three hundred Satan worshipers now entering the auditorium. They say they're going to take over the platform. You can hear them coming now."

The crowd could hear the rising chant of the Satan worshipers. Everyone turned to see them moving with determination down the aisles, past the ushers who were working to restrain them. They were causing a considerable disturbance by that time. I continued addressing the crowd. "I'm going to ask you Christian young people to surround these Satan worshipers," I exhorted. "Love them. Pray for them. Sing to them. And gradually ease them back toward the entrances through which they have come."

I will never forget that moment! Hundreds of young Christians stood to their feet and did exactly as I had asked. Some grabbed hands and began to sing. Others put their arms around the Satan worshipers and began to pray for them. Others calmly shared their faith with them. Everyone else in McCormick Place sat praying as God's Spirit moved through His people to confound the work of Satan in our midst. I stood watching in silence. I waited and prayed until peace was restored and the service could resume.

It happened again in Oakland, California, in the football stadium. Hundreds of Satan worshipers again invaded the meeting to distract and disturb thousands who had come to hear of Christ and His plan of salvation. We did the same thing we had done in Chicago. Again, hundreds of Christians stood and gently led the worshipers of Satan from the stadium. I asked the young people to surround them and to love them. They did! Later that week I received a letter from one of the leaders of the Satanist group thanking me for what I had done. He wrote, "I think you saved our lives." The power of those Christian young people came not in the impact of evil and violent force, but in their quiet, loving, prayerful resolution.

A STORM OF DISCORD

In recent years we have seen some encouraging signs within the churches. Many are growing dramatically, with a surge in Christian megachurches and theologically sound "branch churches" and related parachurch ministries. Evangelical seminaries are bulging at the seams. Countless thousands of small-group Bible studies have sprung up all over the nation. But other reports say that at the same time, there is growing dissatisfaction in recent years—especially among "young urban professionals"—with "traditional Christianity." These people, between the ages of twenty-five and forty, have grown up in an age of discontent and distrust. They have a schooled distrust of "fundamentalism." But they have also witnessed the scandals in the highly visible media church, including promiscuity and the misuse of funds by some television preachers. According to some reports, much of this generation has been "turned off to religion" by the predominantly hedonistic secular culture.

In their bestseller, *Megatrends 2000,* John Naisbitt and Patricia Aburdene reported that religion is on the rise in this generation. They cited a 1987 Gallup poll which showed that 94 percent of Americans believe in God, but they asked, "are Americans 'religious' or 'spiritual'?" (John Naisbitt and Patricia Aburdene, *Megatrends 1000,* 295). Approximately 70 percent of the baby boomers, they say, believe in a "positive, active spiritual force." While the authors say that conservative, Bible-believing churches are growing steadily, they also show that the New Age movement and other "nontraditional" movements are still booming. These authors also relate that, according to the *Encyclopedia of American Religions,* four hundred new religious groups were formed in the United States between 1987 and 1989.

Do such statistics indicate deception or discontent? Again, I would have to say both. Young people and young adults are experimenting with exotic practices and beliefs in the effort to find "unity" with "the force." Millions have been deceived, and where deception exists, disillusionment follows. Disillusionment and deception are the two primary alternatives to true faith in God, and they are the handiwork of the first horseman of the Apocalypse.

The deceiver has many options in his bag of tricks; the first is leading susceptible people to ignore religion altogether. When we feel alienated, isolated, unloved, lonely, and adrift in a cold dark universe, we need God. But the deceiver tells us "there is no God." The nineteenth-century philosopher Friedrich Nietzsche said "God is dead." Do not seek God or Jesus Christ, he whispers, seek escape. I would suggest that this is the real reason why drugs are such an epidemic in America today. This is why promiscuous sex runs rampant, why alcohol abuse is commonplace. Without faith in God, men and women are alone. They will do anything to fill the void in their lives, but short of Christ, nothing works. Augustine said, "Thou madest us for Thyself, and our heart is restless, until it repose in Thee" (*The Confessions of Saint Augustine*, 1:1).

THE NEW AGE

A second form of deception is the substitution of false religions. The rise of the so-called New Age movement over the past twenty-five or thirty years is the best modern example. The New Age is, in fact, another storm warning indicating man's search for "transcendence" without regard for righteousness. Whether it's Dianetics, est, Unity, Gaea, Transcendental Meditation, Taoism, ufology, crystalology, goddess worship, reincarnation, harmonics, numerology, astrology, holistic healing, positive thinking, or any of a hundred "consciousness raising" techniques of our day, the modern age is on a search for some mystical "divine unity," a search which actually testifies to the failure of modern secular humanism to satisfy the spiritual hunger of the soul.

Humanity was designed for a relationship with God. As the body craves oxygen, so the spirit craves God. We all have a passionate desire to know God and to communicate with Him, but ever since Eden we have been guilty of sin, and nothing but repentance—by humbling ourselves before the cross of Christ—will ever bring us back into fellowship with Him.

The real disaster of the cult of humanism and its New Age and other expressions is not just the foolishness of placing one's trust in such a frail, finite, and limited creature but that it separates man from the authentic source of power and meaning. David's lament in Psalm 10 has never been truer than today: "The wicked in his proud countenance does not seek God; God is in none of his thoughts" (Psalm 10:4, NKJV).

Many people have decided that there is no room for God in their lives, no need of Him. The God of Jacob is too confining. The problem, however, is that denying the existence of God cannot make Him go away any more than denying the existence of the Internal Revenue Service makes the tax man go away. Many people who have imagined a god of their own choosing will be horrified when they have to stand before the true God of heaven. For God is, and His is the kingdom and the power and the glory forever. No pious idealism, no New Age fantasy, and no amount of denial can ever change that fact.

Still another ploy of the New Age is to transform God into something else, or to come to the conclusion, as many have done, that we are gods. On the last page of her book, *Out on a Limb,* actress Shirley MacLaine attempts to make herself equal with God when she writes:

I know that I exist, therefore I AM.

I know that the God source exists. Therefore IT IS.

Since I am a part of that force, then I AM that I AM.

In the eyes of a righteous God, there is no greater blasphemy, but such "abomination" has become common heresy in our day. It is one more evidence of the rider on the white horse "going out conquering and to conquer" through his deceptions.

THE WORK OF THE DECEIVER

In this age of humanism, man wants to believe he can become his own god. The remark attributed to Protagoras, that "Man is the measure of all things," is the central tenet of humanist ideology. But it is the ultimate deception of Satan: to rob men of their relationship with the God of the universe through a lie as old as Eden, that "You will be like God" (Genesis 3:5).

Because it springs from false theology, and especially because it is inspired by the deceiver himself, the New Age movement will not bow before God. Rather, it tries to manufacture its own infinitely forgiving and fallible god designed on the pantheistic concept of the oneness of man with the universe. When a Hollywood actress claims to be God, she is simply denying that she has sinned and fallen short of the glory of God. New Agers are terrified by their own mortality, and they want to believe that somehow the soul will survive. Of course it will, but not as they imagine.

Someday the New Age gurus will die, even as we all must die, and their bodies will return to the earth from which God made it. Then what remains, their eternal spirits, will stand before the true and righteous and all-knowing God of creation and explain why they felt compelled to run so hard to escape the God who loved them and gave His Son as a sacrifice. They can explain why, instead, they publicized beliefs which are an abomination in the eyes of a jealous God, and they will hear His reply.

On that day, sincerity will mean nothing; hard work will mean nothing; good intentions will mean nothing. God judges every man, woman, and child by the standard of the only God-Man who ever lived, Jesus Christ. Jesus, the innocent Lamb of God, pledged His innocence for us, to stand between our sin and the judgment of God the Father. Without that holy Shield, no one is worthy. That is the lesson of the fourth chapter of Revelation.

The sin nature is born within each of us; we are not born noble, as Rousseau and the philosophers of the Enlightenment declared. The horseman who brings war testifies to the evil and deceit in our human natures; the terror of war and the storm clouds of holocaust prove that. Left to our own devices, we will destroy the world around us.

Author and writer Russell Chandler, in his book *Understanding the New Age,* reports that dozens of American companies (perhaps unintentionally) are indoctrinating men and women into the New Age movement through "consciousness raising" techniques and required "self-improvement" courses. Many Fortune 500 companies regularly send their executives off to remote training centers and retreats to "get in touch with their inner person." In plain language, that means they are being introduced to such New Age practices as meditation, visual imaging, Zen, yoga, chanting, and even Tarot cards. All this is done in the name of "success enhancement." What it amounts to is opening up the human spirit to the ultimate source of deception: the father of lies.

HOW DECEPTION TAKES HOLD

Why are the cults and the New Age movement so successful today? Why are so many people willing to be swept away by false teaching and thereby are turning their backs on God's truth? There are many reasons, but I am afraid we Christians must confess that at times we have been part of the problem because we are not examples of Christ's love and purity as we should be. Many people—especially young people—have become disillusioned with the Christian faith and the church, and have therefore been open to deception.

This is not a new phenomenon. Throughout history there have been examples of Christian believers becoming unwitting allies of the horseman who deceives. Rather than standing against the symbol of the white horse whose hoofbeats we can hear, unknowingly we can assist him. Sometimes it is in word and action. For example, some churchmen in Nazi Germany gave their official blessing to Hitler's Third Reich as it wreaked havoc on Europe (although others, like Dietrich Bonhoeffer, courageously spoke out and even paid for their courage with their lives). Sometimes our sin comes as a result of our silence and inaction. sins of omission.

Today, too, Christian believers are in danger of helping the rider on the white horse to deceive. In his book, *Unholy Devotion: Why Cults Lure Christians,* Harold Bussell says: "In our fervor to point out [the cult's] errors of doctrine, we have virtually ignored our own shortcomings and vulnerabilities." I will briefly illustrate some of the ways too many people assist in the deception of others through: (1) half-truths, easy answers, and lies; (2) maintaining double standards (saying one thing but doing another); (3) discriminating against certain sins while approving or ignoring other sins; (4) inadequate practical teaching about the "outward journey."

THE NEED FOR CAUTION

One of the primary reasons young people reject Christ and follow after the rider who deceives and his New Age and cultic allies are the half-truths, easy answers, and lies we Christians have sometimes told in our attempts to "sell the faith." I have listened to too many sermons, read too many Christian books, and seen too many Christian films with happily-ever-after endings. Some even declare that if you become a Christian you will get rich or always be successful. This is simply false teaching.

In our attempt to share the faith, some have given the impression that, once a person has accepted Christ as Savior and Lord, his or her problems will be over. That is not true; in fact, it is often quite the opposite. Becoming "new" in Christ is a wonderful beginning, but it isn't the end of pain or problems in our lives. It is the beginning of our facing up to them. Being a Christian involves a lifetime of hard work, dedicated study, and difficult decisions. Christ did not teach that a life of faith would be easy, but that the reward for endurance would be great.

After the apostle Paul's dramatic conversion on the road to Damascus, I doubt if he ever dreamed what hardship and suffering lay ahead. Even though God had told Ananias, who was to disciple Paul, "I will show him how much he must suffer for My name's sake" (Acts 9:16), he could not have known what lay ahead in not only living the Christian life, but in serving Christ. In 2 Corinthians 6, he recounts some of his sufferings, not in discouragement and complaining, but in joy and victory:

In great endurance; in troubles, hardships and distresses; in beatings, imprisonments and riots; in hard work, sleepless nights and hunger; ...through glory and dishonor, bad report and good report; genuine, yet regarded as impostors; known, yet regarded as unknown; dying, and yet we live on; beaten, and yet not killed; sorrowful, yet always rejoicing; poor, yet making many rich; having nothing, and yet possessing everything. (2 Corinthians 6:4–5, 8–10, NIV)

Then the apostle gives even more specific detail. He says:

Three times I was beaten with rods, once I was stoned, three times I was shipwrecked, I spent a night and a day in the open sea, I have been constantly on the move. I have been in danger from rivers, in danger from bandits, in danger from my own countrymen, in danger from Gentiles; in danger in the city, in danger in the country, in danger at sea; and in danger from false brothers. I have labored and toiled and have often gone without sleep; I have known hunger and thirst and have often gone without food; I have been cold and naked. Besides everything else, I face daily the pressure of my concern for all the churches. Who is weak, and I do not feel weak? Who is led into sin, and I do not inwardly burn? If I must boast, I will boast of the things that show my weakness. (2 Corinthians 11:25–30, NIV)

For Paul the Christian life was one of suffering. The same could be said of a multitude of Christ's followers, many of whom were killed for their faith. So when Christ said time after time that one must "deny himself and take up his cross daily and follow me" (Luke 9:23, NIV), He was indicating that it will not always be easy to be His follower. The apostle Paul warned, "Everyone who wants to live a godly life in Christ Jesus will be persecuted" (2 Timothy 3:12, NIV). He offers no cheap grace, no easy life. He did not call for what has been called "easy believism." As someone else has said, "Salvation is free but not cheap."

Charles T. Studd was a famous sportsman in England, captain of the Cambridge XI cricket team. A century ago he gave away his vast wealth to needy causes and led the Cambridge Seven to China. His slogan was, "If Jesus Christ be God and died for me, then no sacrifice can be too great for me to make for Him."

During the first decade of this century, Bill Borden left one of America's greatest family fortunes to be a missionary in China. He only got as far as Egypt where, still in his twenties, he died of typhoid fever. Before his death he said, "No reserves, no retreats, no regrets!"

A generation ago, Jim Elliot went from Wheaton College to become a missionary to the Aucas in Ecuador. Before he was killed, he wrote, "He is no fool who gives up what he cannot keep to gain what he cannot lose." In some parts of the world it is still very hard to be a Christian. In many places men and women are martyred for their faith. At this moment Coptic and Orthodox Christians in the Middle East are undergoing great trials and sufferings. In Latin America, Asia, and in many places in Western Europe, the price of faithful service to Jesus Christ can be humiliation, torture, and death. A 1991 report by Barrett and Johnson shows that more than 40 million Christians have died as martyrs since A.D. 33, including an average of 290,000 Christian martyrs worldwide per year in the 1990s.

In North America it may be just as hard to stand up against the ridicule of secularism and its humanist values. Materialism and self-centeredness are the great vices of our age. But whatever comes your way, know that Christ is in your struggles with you. He knows what it means to suffer, for He, the sinless Son of God, suffered the pangs of death and hell for you. He knows what it means to be tempted, and "Because he himself suffered when he was tempted, he is able to help those who are being tempted" (Hebrews 2:18, NIV). In the midst of every situation of life, He can give an inner calm and strength that you could never imagine apart from Him. "Peace I leave with you," He said, "my peace I give you. I do not give to you as the world gives. Do not let your hearts be troubled and do not be afraid" (John 14:27, NIV). The storms of life will come, but Jesus will be there with you.

The benefits of Christianity are tremendous, but the trials may sometimes seem just as great. So when any preacher or teacher of the Christian gospel oversells either the material or the spiritual benefits of the faith, he is actually aiding the work of the horseman who deceives.

DOUBLE STANDARDS

Another reason the rider who deceives is having a field day in our society is the double standard practiced within some Christian churches. I like the little bumper sticker that reads, "Christians aren't perfect, just forgiven." Christian leaders point their finger at cults and cult leaders and accuse them of deceiving their members. "They say one thing and practice another," the cultists complain.

But perhaps we need to examine our own history as Christian believers. How many Christians today are guilty of the same sin? Too often our Christianity is in our mouths and not in our minds. Which of us cannot identify with the words of the apostle Paul who said, "For the good that I will to do, I do not do; but the evil I will not to do, that I practice" (Romans 7:19, NKJV).

Often the outsider can see through our facades; he calls it hypocrisy. He has heard the stories of Christian churches that have been divided by anger and hatred. He knows about the deacon who left his wife to run away with the church organist. He knows how some of the Sunday morning faithful spend Saturday night. He knows that Christian believers, too, are human. Yet how we work to keep that secret hidden!

We sometimes see Christian books about celebrities who are supposedly converted to the faith. All too often, after the book is released, our celebrity Christian is caught in a front-page scandal. We produce films about the wonderful change Christ makes in a couple facing tragedy. Then, as has happened on occasion, just as the film is released that same couple announces their divorce. Ministers, deacons, Christian leaders, and celebrities are all vulnerable to sin. Why can't we simply face up to these problems openly and deal with them—without excusing them?

As long as we remain in these mortal bodies, none of us will ever be perfect. None of us lives without occasional sin and failure, and it is hypocritical to pretend otherwise. At the same time, however, we must never grow complacent about sin or simply say, "Oh well, everyone else is doing it too." The Bible commands, "But just as he who called you is holy, so be holy in all you do" (1 Peter 1:15, NIV). It also tells us that there is forgiveness and new life when we repent and confess our sins to Christ.

WASHED WHITER THAN SNOW

My wife told me a story about the early mountain people in the area where we live who used to have a wooden cradle with slatted sides to put their laundry in. The cradle was placed crossways in a rushing creek, and as the water flowed through the slats, the laundry was continuously cleansed. Ruth laughed, this was probably the first automatic washing machine in North Carolina. One day a bootlegger in our area was converted. When he was taken down to the stream to be baptized, he asked if he could please be put crossways to the current so that he would "get washed the cleaner!"

When sin and failure come in our lives, as they most certainly will, we still have the wonderful promise that "the blood of Jesus, his Son, purifies us from all sin" (1 John 1:7, NIV). That promise was written to believers. And the word used here, *purifies* (or, in the King James Version *cleanseth*), means "continuous cleansing."

The greatest thing you can do when you have sinned is to go immediately to the Scriptures and claim the many promises of God. Memorize some of them. Psalm 119:11 (KJV) says, "Thy word have I hid in mine heart, that I might not sin against thee." Because it was inspired by God for imperfect human beings, Scripture has the remedy for sinfulness.

Another thing I have found helpful is to confide in a very close Christian friend who can share your burden, problem, or failure in confidence. I would add a word of caution here, however. There are some believers in whom you may confide who cannot wait to tell someone else. Use caution in choosing friends, counselors, and confidants, but don't let fear be an excuse for hiding your secrets from a Christian brother or sister. Just be sure you can trust the one to whom you talk. Then ask that person to read the Scripture and pray with you.

Why must we pretend with each other? Why should we wear assumed smiles of victory in our public gatherings and weep tears

of loneliness and anger when we are alone? If your business fails
and bankruptcy threatens, let your brother and sister in Christ be
aware of your struggle. If your marriage is coming apart at the
seams, find at least one or two trustworthy believers to share your
pain and help you deal in practical ways with the problems you
face. The Bible says, "Carry each other's burdens, and in this way
you will fulfill the law of Christ" (Galatians 6:2, NIV).

It only takes one act of repentance to receive Christ as Lord
and Savior. But repentance is not a onetime act. All Christians are
guilty of individual and corporate sin. Corporate sin is participat-
ing in a group's sin, whether it's a family that ignores a neighbor
in need, a church that ignores the needs of its neighborhood, or a
nation that ignores the demands of a holy and righteous God.

FREEDOM IN FORGIVENESS

Once we confess the fact that we Christians, too, still sin, we see
unbelievers in a new light, and they will see us in a new light. We
do not look down on their sinfulness from any position of arro-
gance. We simply reach out in understanding and in love, offering
to our fellow sinners the forgiveness and new life that we were
freely given in Christ. When we admit that we are not perfect, just
forgiven, and share the Scriptures, we drive away the rider who
deceived. But as long as we pretend to be perfect and live behind
the double standard, we give him room to ride.

Let us pray that God will make us sensitive to sin wherever it
is found. We must reach out in Christian love to those whose lives
are battered and bruised by sin, point them to the only One who
can bring healing and new life, and welcome them into our fellowship. "For it is God's will that by doing good you should
silence the ignorant talk of foolish men. Live as free men, but do

not use your freedom as a cover-up for evil; live as servants of God" (1 Peter 2:15–16, NIV).

The inward journey is that lifelong pilgrimage of spiritual growth and maturity in the life of the believer. Many times pastors and Christian leaders tend to see conversion as the end rather than the beginning of life's struggle to know God and to do His will. Going forward in a crusade or church to receive Jesus Christ as Lord and Savior is really just the first step of the inward journey.

Ultimately this journey should include such things as daily study of God's Word, the practice of prayer, the reading of Christian books and articles, memorization of Bible verses, gathering together with other believers in a sound Bible-believing church, participation in small mentoring or Bible study groups, and building intimate and honest Christian friendships. All of these activities are necessary if we are to grow in the Christian faith. We must not assume that people understand and practice these disciplines on their own. They need direction and encouragement, and in many cases they need leadership.

I'll never forget a pastor telling me the story of one of his most faithful members who did not know how to pray. She had been a hard-working, committed member of the church since her conversion in a crusade. She had taught Sunday school and pledged her financial support. She had even brought neighbors and friends to church. One Wednesday evening the pastor asked the woman to lead in a closing prayer. After a long, embarrassing silence she ran from the room in tears. For a while the woman disappeared. She wouldn't answer her phone. She didn't return to church. Finally she called the pastor and made an appointment to see him. In his study, the woman confessed that she didn't know how to pray. She didn't know what to say or how to say it. Everyone had just assumed that she could pray, but she honestly didn't know how.

The pastor told me that teaching this person from a totally secular background how to pray was one of the most difficult and rewarding tasks of his ministry. By walking her through the elements of a simple, heartfelt prayer, he helped her gain new and intimate access to the very throne of God. The experience gave new meaning to the disciples' request directed to Jesus, "'Lord, teach us to pray, just as John taught his disciples'" (Luke 11:1, NIV).

THE MOMENT OF INNOCENCE

Each evening in our crusades, I give the invitation for people to commit themselves to Christ. Afterward I talk to them about four important things that must be part of their lives if they are to develop and mature. One of those is prayer. I tell them that they may not be able to pray like a clergyman in the beginning, but they can start with just a simple sentence. "Lord, I love you." That's a prayer. Or, "God, help me." That's a prayer. Since the disciples had to be taught to pray, we, too, ought to study the Scriptures and learn to pray.

Christian leaders would do well to recognize that the term "babes in Christ" has a very specific meaning. There is an innocence and vulnerability in many new believers that the deceiver will exploit if we allow him. If we do not continue to teach Christian principles to the new believers, we run the risk of simply opening their eyes to spiritual issues so that cults or other influences can take over. In contrast, cult leaders sweep down upon their converts and offer them rigorous spiritual discipline. While we are taking for granted that all is well with the new converts, cults assume that their new members know nothing. They start from scratch and build into the newcomer all the skills he or she needs to feel a part of that particular cultic system.

By assuming too much, we can leave these infant believers open and vulnerable to New Age spiritualism with its sophisticated systems and pat answers or to other kinds of modern "isms" that can quickly overcome the truth they have so newly gained. It is important for local church leaders to keep in touch with the spiritual state of their members, to discuss their level of biblical knowledge, or to determine how well and how often people pray.

A recent survey showed that 85 percent of the seminaries of this country had no classes on prayer. How many local churches offer classes on developing the skill and practice of prayer? One church had a "week of waiting," an *entire week for prayer!* The rider who deceives gloats when we assume our people are alive and growing. He is all too free to ride into our ranks and to make victims of us all if and when our inward journey, our spiritual growth and maturity, are not a primary concern to us all.

THE OUTWARD JOURNEY

The outward journey is an expression that I think originated with Elizabeth O'Connor, the historian of the Church of the Savior in Washington, D.C. To grow on an inward journey, the journey to know God, is not enough. We are also called to follow Christ onto our streets and into our neighborhoods. We are called to serve Christ in bringing His message of redemption to the world. The outward journey, which takes us beyond our own small world to the world in need, is the inevitable outworking of a genuine inward journey. The Great Commission of Christ points in two directions: toward God and toward our neighbors.

The Church of the Savior requires that each member be

actively working in some sort of outreach project, whether it be evangelism through a Bible study; a retreat ministry; rebuilding houses or feeding the poor; caring for orphans, widows, and transients; being involved in the primary concerns of education; public housing; or environment. That is an exceptional requirement for membership, but to require people to be effective ambassadors of Christ is not at all unrealistic. I wish more churches would consider this option. Sometimes we act as if attending church on Sunday morning and putting an offering in the basket is all that God requires of us. That sort of church is little more than a picnic or an amusement. It makes the faith seem like an empty ritual; "It makes me feel good." We forget Jesus standing before the rich young man saying, "Sell everything you have and give to the poor...Then come, follow me" (Mark 10:21, NIV).

The rider who deceives revels when we make faith seem too easy. Faith involves trust and commitment. The crowd at the fringe of the cross is easily led away. But those who mix their blood and sweat with the tears of the martyrs are not easily deceived. The more involved a believer is in a daily devotional life and in the lives and needs of others, the more he or she will grow in faith and in practice. The less involved, the more likely he or she is to be deceived.

Many sincere people leave the church and join the cults because the cults make demands. When committing their lives to a belief or cause, people expect a challenge. People respond to the call to hardship. The cults offer practical ways that the followers can serve others, while churches often talk about "cross bearing" but never give their members the sorts of practical, sometimes difficult tasks that make Christian service practical and rewarding. It may seem ironic, but if we don't make demands, the rider who deceives will rein in and provide practical programs of caring as the first step of deception.

WHO WON THE SHOWDOWN IN THE DESERT?

RON MEHL

Ron Mehl
Pastor, speaker, author

Then Jesus, being filled with the Holy Spirit, returned
from the Jordan and was led by the Spirit into the wilderness, being tempted for forty days by the devil. And in
those days He ate nothing, and afterward, when they had
ended, He was hungry. And the devil said to Him, "If You
are the Son of God, command this stone to become
bread." But Jesus answered him, saying, "It is written,
'Man shall not live by bread alone, but by every word of God.'"
Then the devil, taking Him up on a high mountain,
showed Him all the kingdoms of the world in a moment
of time. And the devil said to Him, "All this authority I
will give You, and their glory; for this has been delivered
to me, and I give it to whomever I wish. Therefore, if You
will worship before me, all will be Yours." And Jesus
answered and said to him, "Get behind Me, Satan! For it
is written, *'You shall worship the LORD your God, and Him
only you shall serve.'*" Then he brought Him to Jerusalem,

set Him on the pinnacle of the temple, and said to Him, "If You are the Son of God, throw Yourself down from here. For it is written: *'He shall give His angels charge over you, to keep you,'* and, *'In their hands they shall bear you up, lest you dash your foot against a stone.'"* And Jesus answered and said to him, "It has been said, *'You shall not tempt the LORD your God.'"* (Luke 4:1–12, NKJV)

Part of the reason they pay professional baseball players so much is to answer worn-out questions from would-be baseball analysts.

I was speaking in Seattle not long ago, when I was introduced to Pete O'Brien, first baseman for the Seattle Mariners.

He probably heard something click in my head as we shook hands.

He probably knew what was coming.

"You know, Pete, there are just one or two *little* things I've always wanted to ask someone like you."

"Oh,...really?"

Pete was gracious. I popped up a few questions and he was willing to field them.

"Do you guys, umm, pretty well know the different pitchers' styles—I mean, what they'll throw in different situations?"

"Pretty well," he said.

"Do they know *you?*"

"Oh, yeah. They know the strengths and weaknesses of every batter they'll face. They know if you're a great fastball hitter, or if you're a terrible curveball hitter."

"They know all that?"

"Oh, sure. They keep a book on everyone—your hitting average, home runs, strike outs, and what pitches you'll swing at in a given situation."

"No kidding!"

"Yeah, and then at the crucial point—when the game is on the line—the pitcher and catcher have a quick summit meeting. The pitcher says, 'I think this guy probably *thinks* I'm going to throw a curveball. He knows that I know he's a terrible curveball hitter. I think he'll be anticipating a curveball.' Assuming the batter will be looking to guard his weakness, the pitcher decides to go right at the batter's strength, a high fastball."

That conversation with my new friend flashed across my mind a few weeks ago as I studied Luke 4.

Two thousand years ago, a lonely Nazarene carpenter stepped up to the plate at a crucial moment. But it wasn't just a game on the line—*everything* was on the line. Your eternal destiny and mine. Salvation for the whole world. Unimaginable implications stretching into endless ages.

What did hell's book of statistics have that day on a famished young Jew named Jesus? With all the forces of darkness cheering Him on, what would the pitcher throw at Him?

It would seem prudent that he throw his best stuff. They say, "It's three strikes and you're out." Hell's starting pitcher threw several pitches at our Lord—all designed to challenge the most basic and essential areas of human need. As a result of this head-to-head duel, the potential results of all other battles yet to be waged would be decided.

When it comes to temptation, every person will have his or her time at bat. There are no designated hitters to stand in for us. We all will enter the batter's box alone. Satan is so desperate to win he'll throw whatever it takes to "get us outta there." He doesn't know everything about us, but he does know where we're weak.

In any book about Good Things and Bad Things, temptation has to be one of the *worst* things. Look back through history at the strike outs. From Adam and Eve to King Solomon to Judas Iscariot. Untold horrors—all the incomprehensible evils since the Fall—have occurred when men and women succumbed to temptation.

A very Bad Thing.

But then...Jesus was tempted.

And did not strike out.

And calmly faced the worst hellfire fastballs Satan could hurl and came through it all with power and glory and a rock-hard commitment to walk His Father's path.

And that was a Good Thing. I can't even tell you how good.

So which is it for you and me? Can this most dreadful Bad Thing become for us a Good Thing?

Perhaps the first step to answering that question is to get a better handle on what this phenomenon is all about.

Just what is temptation?

WHAT TEMPTATION IS

Temptation, at its core, is a shortcut.

It's the fast track to quick results. Satan's strategy against Christians usually suggests we do three things: move quickly, think shallowly, and invest ourselves deeply.

When we *move quickly* we are prone to surrender to unbridled desires of the flesh. The flesh is driven by sudden urges and fleeting passions, not by deliberate convictions.

When we *think shallowly* we don't take the time to weigh and consider the ramifications or consequences of our choices.

When we *invest ourselves deeply* in an action, attitude, or thought pattern it becomes increasingly difficult to withdraw.

Temptation masquerades as better, quicker, and easier, but is in the end a more expensive and painful way. Its offerings are deceptive and always second best. From steriods to premarital sex to cheating on Wall Street, temptation looks, sounds, and feels good on the surface. But beneath its facade, the reward is *short-term* and the consequences are *long-term.*

I've always been drawn by shortcuts. I can recall a summer morning many years ago when Mom called me to the kitchen just as I was heading out the door with my baseball and mitt.

"Son," she said, "would you please go and dig the dandelions? They're beginning to take over the front yard."

Now I loved my mom and would do anything she asked, but…when you're eleven years old and playing baseball is your dream for the day, the prospect of two or three hours in a dande-lion patch is a terrible come-down.

From the field of dreams to a field of weeds.

It was really almost more than a boy could bear.

I dragged myself out the door, flopped down on the front lawn, picked up the knife, and dug up two or three. The pesky things had roots like a redwood. After what seemed like an hour, I looked up to gaze over the yard…a veritable sea of yellow blos-soms. There must have been *hundreds* of those things, their little golden heads bobbing in unison to the summer breeze. Despair filled my heart. *This is gonna take all day!* I told myself.

That's when I came up with my short cut.

I simply crawled the length of our yard and pulled off all the flowers. The whole thing hardly took more than twenty minutes. Mom was pleased and impressed.

A few days later, however, a vast ocean of yellow lapped at the front porch and back patio. The dandelions were not only back, they had multiplied ten-fold. And I had some serious explaining to do.

That's the way it is with shortcuts. They rarely deal with the root of the problem. They're cosmetic, and may look good for the moment, but what seems so good ends up so bad.

WHAT TEMPTATION DOES

Temptation, like a great crowbar, seeks to lever people away from their God-given responsibilities and bar their way to the Lord's rich and lasting rewards. Ephesians 5 and 6 suggest spiritual warfare rages in predictable places: our responsibilities to our families, our ministries in the church, and our service on the job. It is little wonder we see a breakdown of the family, division in the church, and dissension on the job. If Satan can succeed in prying us away from our personal responsibilities, he creates a gaping hole in God's protective covering over our lives that leaves us—as well as those around us—vulnerable to his attack.

If we really stop and think about it for a moment, Satan often offers us things that are already ours...*if we are willing to wait and trust God for them*. In the wilderness Satan challenged Jesus to prove His power—yet He's the Creator of the universe. Satan offered Jesus prominence—yet He's the King of kings and Lord of lords.

In the beginning, Adam and Eve were blessed with authority, position, and power. God had glorious plans for their lives. Little wonder they were so severely seduced by the devil. Seeing that the forbidden tree was good for food, Eve took of the fruit, hoping it would make her wise. This deadly shortcut cost them their lives, their joy, their relationship with God, and—really more than we can begin to comprehend.

God promised Abraham a son from union with his barren wife, Sarah. But then the patriarch took a shortcut with Sarah's maid, Hagar. Abraham was *still* going to have a son by Sarah. But now he would have to wait ten more years...and deal with the consequences of his impatience for the rest of his life.

Esau was a man who yielded to the desires of the flesh and became its slave so that even his birthright, which was a valuable, precious gift from God, didn't have as much meaning to him as a bowl of stew to satisfy a moment's gnawing hunger.

The voice of the tempter continually whispers, "Take it now...indulge yourself now...get your satisfaction now...make your big play now...grab your pleasure now."

I'm reminded of all the radio and TV commercials that sprout up like so many dandelions between January and April. Lending institutions offer to loan people the exact amount of their tax return. Why? So they won't have to wait for a few weeks to spend it! "Why wait for Uncle Sam's check in the mail?" the announcers ask. "Go out and get that boat now. Take that cruise now. Buy those new clubs now. Build that deck now."

Funny that they never mention the interest rate.

The Ultimate Loan Shark doesn't either. But don't kid yourself. Satan's interest rate is extremely high. It adds up quickly. It compounds daily. Before you know it, he owns you.

I counsel many young people who have listened to the slick ads of the Loan Shark. *You want sex now?* He whispers. *Take it. I'll advance you whatever you want. Enjoy yourself. Go for it. Do it now. Don't worry about my fees. We'll talk about that later on.*

And "later on" is when they come into my office. Broken.

Stripped of their innocence. Used up. Rejected. Racked by guilt. Ripped apart by regret. Suicidal.

While sex within the confines of marriage is a proper and pleasurable experience, Satan offers to advance us the erotic pleasures at an *improper* time. And the people I've talked to always discover they've only cheated themselves. When they finally get what they think they wanted, they find it didn't fulfill their needs. They lost far more than they gained.

I know a godly and lovely young woman who struggled with being single. She came to believe that her fulfillment, joy, and contentment would come only through marriage. She looked and looked, waited and waited, with no results. Soon, in her desire to satisfy her need for companionship, she decided that *anything is better than nothing.* So she vowed to marry the next Available Male.

It was just seven months after her wedding with Mr. Available that she came weeping into my office. "Oh, how I wish I was lonely again!" she sobbed. "It would be a lot better than THIS! I didn't realize how good I had it!"

Most of the mistakes we make happen when we hurry and don't think. That's why the advertising agencies of the world spend billions to determine the best way to approach us. They concentrate on our sexual passions, our curiosity, and need to succeed. Working through our emotions, they prod us to make quick, impulsive decisions.

The world says that the shortest route to personal fulfillment is to discover our deepest desires and satisfy them. But feeding an appetite only makes it crave more! In fact, the Book of Ephesians speaks of uncleanness and greediness in the same breath. It's clear that we can *never* satisfy our own fleshly desires. Just try eating one M&M!

The desires of our flesh may appear at times to be only an innocent trickle. But soon, if fed, they become an uncontrollable torrent. You can't overcome the flesh by saying yes, but only saying no. As Paul said, "I discipline my body and bring it into subjection" (1 Corinthians 9:27, NKJV).

The media in the Pacific Northwest recently reported a horrifying accident. A rural Oregon couple was keeping a rare liger in a cage in their garage. A liger is the offspring of a tiger and a lion. Not a tame kitty by any stretch of the imagination. Another family was visiting, and went out to the garage to look at the ferocious animal. For some incomprehensible reason, the visiting parents allowed their twelve-year-old daughter to stray near the cage, and actually reach her arm inside to pet the beast. Instantly the big cat sank its teeth deep into the girl's arm and shoulder *and would not let go.* Everyone was screaming and beating the animal with whatever they could find, but the teeth were clamped down like a bloody vise. It took a bullet through the animal's brain to release its iron grip.

That's our flesh. You cannot coddle and tame it. It's quick and greedy and cruel. It has iron jaws. It hangs on and will not let go.

The flesh is like a wild animal, and you'd be well warned to never turn your back on it. It's unpredictable…you're never sure what it's going to do. It will put up with anything until you mess with its food. The moment you stop feeding it, it rises up.

When you corner a panther and face it head-on, it will lie down like a gentle lamb and pretend the confrontation is no big deal. But never turn your back on it because, if given the chance, it will attack in an unguarded moment. The reason some people don't fall during times of temptation is because they *realize* they *can* fall. They acknowledge and face the weakness of their own flesh.

Unfortunately, most of us learn by experience. No matter how mature you become, you must always remember your flesh will never be weakened or tamed. It must always be dealt with.

How Did Jesus Handle Temptation?

A good question to ask ourselves when faced with seasons of temptation is this: What was the Lord thinking when He faced such savage testing in the wilderness.

Forty days and forty nights is quite a stretch. That leaves lots of time for thinking. What might have been going through His mind? How did He pass the time? I know what I would do. I'd cry and complain, question and complain, get discouraged and complain. But what might Jesus have done? What did He contemplate?

Isn't it likely He was pondering the work of His Father in the wilderness throughout man's history?

Wouldn't He have recalled how He and His Father, with the Holy Spirit, sent Abraham into the wilderness to the mountain of Moriah with instructions to sacrifice his cherished son, Isaac? Wouldn't He have remembered how Abraham responded without question, believing that if he had to kill his boy God would raise Isaac from the dead? Might not Jesus, in *His* wilderness, have recalled the desolation, loneliness, and agony of that moment?

At bleak, barren Moriah, there had been nothing to distract Abraham from total dependence on God. The test pressed the old patriarch to his limits and beyond. It powerfully sharpened his character, molding him by the hand of the Almighty into a giant of a man, the father of faith.

Second, it's obvious from His answers to Satan that Jesus was meditating on the Book of Deuteronomy. Wouldn't He have been thinking about the wilderness wanderings of the Israelites? Wouldn't He have remembered how He and His Father, by the Holy Spirit, had protected and fed and nurtured the Israelites, leading them by a pillar of cloud by day and a pillar of fire by night? Israel's forty-year sojourn in the wilderness was a time of testing—to see whether they would obey God or not. Jesus walked those same sands for forty days—enduring a distilled, concentrated time of satanic testing we can't begin to comprehend.

The wilderness was a place for the awesome revelation of God's power and might. It was a time for all the nations to learn that Jehovah was the true God over all the earth. It was also a time for the demonstration of God's faithfulness to His covenant people. In the face of repeated unbelief and hardness of heart, the world would come to know that even though man may be unfaithful, God remains faithful.

Might He not have remembered how His ancestor David fled into the wilderness to hide from the murderous attacks of Saul? Wouldn't He have recalled the songs of Jesse's son...psalms composed under star-strewn desert skies, in the black depths of limestone caves, or in the shadow of towering rocks in the lonesome afternoons? Can you see His sun-cracked lips moving, silently forming the words through the long hours of testing?

> In the shadow of Your wings
> I will make my refuge,
> Until these calamities have passed by...
>
> For in the time of trouble
> He shall hide me in His pavilion;

In the secret place of His tabernacle
He shall hide me;
He shall set me high upon a rock...

You are my hiding place;
You shall preserve me from trouble;
You shall surround me with songs of deliverance.

Certainly Jesus would have found God's Word to be a pavilion of comfort during those days of pressure and nights of distress.

He would have reflected that the wilderness was a place of security rather than a place of barrenness and death. He would have realized that intense fellowship with His Father in a season of deep trouble and testing was a thing to embrace rather than shun.

One more thing. Could He have been thinking of you and me?

Might He not have thought about the privilege He'd have in the future to encourage us as we face our God-appointed times of testing? If He had not endured during those fierce hours of confrontation with Hell, how could the writer of Hebrews have penned these words?

Seeing then that we have a great High Priest who has passed through the heavens, Jesus the Son of God, let us hold fast our confession. For we do not have a High Priest who cannot sympathize with our weaknesses, but was in all points tempted as we are, yet without sin. Let us therefore come boldly to the throne of grace, that we may obtain mercy and find grace to help in time of need. (Hebrews 4:14–16, NKJV)

It was a Bad Thing and a Good Thing.

It was the best of times and the worst of times.

It was Hell and Heaven in close proximity.

It was utter loneliness and indescribable fellowship.

Through it all the Lord Jesus experienced the delivering hand of His Father. He experienced a hardening of purpose. When He was finished He would go forth in power and work this same hardening of purpose in the lives of His saints. And, unlike Israel, God's servant of old, Jesus proved Himself faithful to the Lord's purposes.

Jesus knew well how the wilderness in our lives is a preamble to joy and blessing when we trust in Him.

> Then Jesus returned in the power of the Spirit to Galilee, and the news of Him went out through all the surrounding region.

It's the power of God that we so desperately need. The Lord's journey on earth took Him to the wilderness. He knew that while none of us are called to live in the wilderness, we may be asked to visit for a season.

Why is the wilderness so important to God? Scripture brims with accounts of the conflicts of men and women in the wilderness and barren lands. The wilderness shows man the truth of who he is. It peels away his pride. Pride is a horrible disease which goes unchecked in this world. Pride convinces man of the strength of his thighs and the maturity of his mind, while blinding him to the strength of the One who has created all things. Pride blinds us all, but the wilderness removes the mask of pride's lying nature and allows man to see himself for who he really is.

There is no cure for pride outside of Christ.

It is God alone in His mercy who sends us out into the wilderness to learn again the first principles. He is the Creator of all that is, and in Him and Him alone all creation lives, and moves, and has its being. All creation is utterly dependent upon Him for the life He has granted each of us.

The wilderness of temptation forces me to acknowledge the power and care of the Almighty God.

It's a place without the noise of the many voices that would draw us away from the plan of God for our lives.

It's a place of deep resolution and often where the deep convictions which mold our lives in God take shape and find their expression.

The Lord stands as a sentry watching the comings and goings of the Christian's daily walk. If God has led you to the wilderness, He will provide a way through the temptation. Nothing you face will be more than He knows you are capable of dealing with, even though it may seem so at times.

Have you ever had the opportunity to watch a baseball game played by the deaf? I think you'd find it fascinating. They can't hear, so hollering positions and instructions just won't work. During the game—especially the crucial moments—you'll see every player on the field fasten his eyes on the coach. The concentration is incredible. Only with their eyes locked on the coach and his hand signals can they be certain they won't miss a key play or muff a personal assignment. They get all their direction and orders from him.

In the same way, we must keep our eyes on our Lord to remain steadfast. If a Bad Thing such as a temptation compels us to rivet our attention on Him, it's a Good Thing.

If you have to bat against the devil, you'd best keep your eye on the Coach's box. He knows every pitch.

He's seen it all before.

THE BATTLE BETWEEN
THE KINGDOMS

CHARLES W. COLSON

Charles W. Colson
Founder and Chairman of Prison Fellowship Ministries
1993 Recipient of Templeton Prize for Progressive Religion
Author, speaker, columnist

I die the king's good servant, but God's first.
—Sir Thomas More

If I am faced with the choice between religion and my country...I will choose my fatherland.
—Father Miguel d'Escoto, Nicaraguan Foreign Minister

Wilberforce's dogged campaign to rid the British empire of the slave trade shows what can happen when a citizen of the Kingdom of God challenges corrupt structures within the kingdoms of man. One excellent Wilberforce biography is aptly titled God's Politician, and truly he was, holding his country to God's standard of moral accountability.

The kind of conflict that Wilberforce and other activist Christians experience—between their Christian conscience and their political mandates—is unavoidable. Both church and state assert standards and values in society; both seek authority; both compete for allegiance. As members of both the religious and the political spheres, the Christian is bound to face conflict.

The conflict is particularly apparent in the Judeo-Christian tradition because of the assertion that the God of both the Old and New Testament Scriptures is King. That has been an offense to the proud and powerful since the beginning—and the reason Jews and Christians alike have been systematically persecuted.

The tension between the Kingdom of God and the kingdoms of man runs like an unbroken thread through the history of the past two thousand years. It began not long after Christ's birth. Herod, the Roman-appointed king over the Jews and as vicious a tyrant as ever lived, was gripped with fear when the Magi arrived from the East seeking the "King of the Jews." Though not a believer, Herod knew the ancient Jewish prophecies that a child would be born to reign over them, ushering in a Kingdom of peace and might.

Herod called the Magi to his ornate throne room. In what has become common practice in the centuries since, he tried to manipulate the religious leaders for political advantage. He told them to go find this King in Bethlehem so he too could worship Him.

The rest of the story is familiar. The Magi found Jesus but were warned in a dream to avoid Herod and return to the East. Jesus' parents, similarly warned, escaped with their son to Egypt—just ahead of Herod's marauding soldiers who massacred all the male children of Jesus' age in and near Bethlehem.

Herod didn't fear Jesus because he thought He would become a religious or political leader. He had suppressed such opponents before. Herod feared Christ because He represented a Kingdom greater than his own.

Jesus was later executed for this same reason. Though He told Pilate His Kingdom was not of this world, the sign over His cross read "INRE"—King of the Jews. The executioner's sarcasm was double-edged.

His followers' faithfulness to Christ's announcement of His kingdom led to their persecution as well. An enraged mob in Thessalonica threatened Paul and Silas, shouting. "These men who have caused trouble all over the world...are all defying Caesar's decrees, saying that there is another king, one called Jesus."[1] During the early centuries Christians were martyred not for religious reasons—Rome, after all, was a land of many gods—but because they refused to worship the emperor. Because they would not say, "We have no king but Caesar," the Roman government saw them as political subversives.

Christians who refused to offer incense before the statue of the emperor were flogged, stoned, imprisoned, condemned to the mines. Later, when Christianity was officially outlawed, they were tortured mercilessly and fed to the lions, to the delight of bloodthirsty crowds.[2]

With the conversion of Constantine, however, Christianity was legalized in A.D. 313. This marked the end of persecution and ushered in a second phase in church-state relations.[3] In A.D. 381 Christianity became the official religion of Rome, and in an ironic turnabout, church leaders began exploiting their new-found power. As historian F. F. Bruce has written: "Christian leaders...exploit[ed] the influential favor they enjoyed even when it meant subordinating the cause of justice to the apparent interest of their religion...they were inclined to allow the secular power too much control in church affairs...Where church leaders were able to exercise political as well as spiritual authority, they did not enjoy any marked immunity from the universally corrupting tendency of power."[4]

Even Augustine, the great church father who provided the classic definition of the roles of the City of God and the city of man, was beguiled by the lure of temporal power; after a wrenching internal struggle he endorsed the suppression of heretics by the state.

Through succeeding centuries the church relied increasingly on the state to punish heresy. By the time of the Byzantine empire in the East, the state had become a theocracy with the church serving as its department of spiritual affairs. In the West both church and state jockeyed for control in an uneasy alliance. In the thirteenth century, for example, Frederick II, king of Sicily, was first excommunicated for not going on a crusade, then excommunicated for going on one without the Pope's permission. The state conquered territory, but the Pope distributed the land to the more faithful crusaders.

The consequences of this alliance were mixed. Certainly Christianity provided a civilizing influence on Western culture through art, music, literature, morality, and ultimately in government. One eminent historian concluded that "society developed only so fast as religion enlarged its sphere."[5] On the darker side however, the excesses of the politicized church created horrors Augustine could not have imagined.

The church turned to military conquest through a series of "holy wars" that became more racial than religious. Jews, Muslims, and dark-skinned Christians were massacred alike. The goal was not to convert the populace, but to conquer it.

In the twelfth and thirteenth centuries a system was organized for adjudicating heresy. Like many well-intentioned reforms, however, the Inquisition simply produced a new set of horrors. Unrepentant heretics were cast out by a church tribunal, which regularly used torture, and were executed by the state.

The spiritual corruption of the church led to the Reformation of the sixteenth century, which produced several streams of church-state relations. One, believing the state to be essentially coercive and violent, rejected participation in any form of government. A second strand of Reformation thought dictated that the religion of a resident king or prince would be the church of the state. Thus, many kings became their own pope. A third principle encouraged church independence. Scottish church leaders like Samuel Rutherford revived the biblical view that God's law reigns over man and his kingdoms. This profoundly influenced the experiment in constitutional government then beginning in the New World.

A new phase of hostility between church and state began in the eighteenth century when waves of skepticism washed over the continent of Europe. Voltaire, one of the most influential philosophers of the day, was vehemently dedicated to the extirpation of what he called "this infamous superstition."

Religions had been assaulted before but always in the name of other religions. With the French Revolution, Tocqueville noted, "Passionate and persistent efforts were made to wean men away from the faith of their fathers...Irreligion became an all-prevailing passion, fierce, intolerant and predatory."[6] For a time this all-prevailing passion was successful. Wrote Tocqueville: "The total rejection of any religious belief, so contrary to man's natural instincts and so destructive of his peace of mind, came to be regarded by the masses as desirable."[7] The French Revolution was a conscious effort to replace the Kingdom of God with the kingdoms of man.

But the state must have some moral justification for its authority. Thus France's irreligion was soon replaced by a new faith—man's worship of man.

Against this backdrop Wilberforce and other heirs of John Wesley's Great Awakening in England brought the Christian conscience to bear on a society that was nominally Christian but engaged in vile practices. Their stand strengthened the church in England at the very moment it was under its most vicious assault.

Meanwhile, in the New World a radical experiment opened another chapter in church-state relations. There a group of gentlemen farmers, who were neither naive about human nature nor pretentious about human society, were drawing up the American Constitution. By refusing to assign redemptive powers to the state or to allow coercive power to the church, the American experiment separated these two institutions for the first time since Constantine.

What might be considered the modern phase in church-state history has emerged in our century. It is an amalgam of elements from the previous eras. The rise of totalitarian regimes has brought back the kind of persecution the church experienced in early Rome; like Herod, modern dictators tolerate no other kings. In the West secularism has aggressively spread irreligion, turning Europe into a post-Christian culture and America into a battleground with orthodox religion in retreat.

Can we conclude from this cursory overview that the church and the state must inevitably be in conflict? To some extent the answer is yes. Dual allegiances always create tension. And in a sinful world the struggle for power, which inevitably corrupts, is unavoidable. When the church isn't being persecuted, it is being corrupted. So as much as anything else, it is man's own nature that has created centuries of conflict.

But every generation has an obligation to seek anew a healthy relationship between church and state. Both are reflections of man's nature; both have a role to play. Christ's teaching clearly delineates these roles.

Jesus was remarkably indifferent to chose who held political power. He had no desire to replace Caesar or Pilate with His apostles Peter or John. He gave civil authority its due, rebuking both the Zealots and Peter for using the sword.

This infuriated the religious right of His day. Eager to discredit Jesus, the Pharisees and Herodians tried trapping Him over the question of allegiance to political authority.

"Tell us," the asked, "is it right to pay taxes to Caesar or not?"

The question put Jesus in the middle: if He said no, He would be a threat to the Roman government; if He said yes, He would lose the respect of the masses who hated the Romans.

Jesus asked them for a coin. It was a Roman denarius, the only coin that could be used to pay the hated yearly poll tax. On one side was the image of the Emperor Tiberius, around which were written the words *Tiberius Caesar Augustus, son of the divine Augustus.*

"Whose portrait is this?" He asked, rubbing His finger over the raised features of the Roman ruler. "And whose inscription?"

"Caesar's," they replied impatiently.

"Give to Caesar what is Caesar's and to God what is God's." replied Jesus, handing the coin back to them. They stared at Him in stunned silence.

Not only had he eluded the trap, but He had put Caesar in his place. Christ might simply have said, "Give to Caesar what is Caesar's." That's all that was at issue. It was Caesar's image on the coin, and Caesar had authority over the state.

What made Him add the second phrase, "Give…to God what is God's"?

The answer, I believe, is found on the reverse face of the coin, which showed Tiberius's mother represented as the goddess of peace, along with the words *highest priest.* The blasphemous words commanded the worship of Caesar; they thus exceeded the state's authority.

Jesus' lesson was not lost on the early church. Government is to be respected, and its rule honored. "It is necessary to submit to the authorities," wrote the apostle Paul. "If you owe taxes, pay taxes."[8] But worship is reserved solely for God.

The distinction Christ made is clear, both church and state have clear and distinct roles ordained by God. The issue is now to apply these teachings to each institution in today's volatile world.

"Christ did not give the keys of the Kingdom to Caesar nor the sword to Peter," writes a contemporary scholar.[9] In God's provision the state is not to seize authority over ecclesiastical or spiritual matters, nor is the church to seek authority over political matters. Yet the constant temptation of each is to encroach upon the other.

Governments, with rare exceptions, seek to expand their power beyond the mandate to restrain evil, preserve order, and promote justice. Most often they do this by venturing into religious or moral areas. The reason is twofold: the state needs religious legitimization for its policies and an independent church is the one structure that rivals the state's claim for ultimate allegiance.

A contemporary example, though admittedly extreme, is the Soviet Union and its Act of 1918 on separation of church and state. This sounds benign enough, but what the Soviets decreed, reinforced in the 1929 law and in subsequent constitutions, is that churches may conduct worship services when licensed by the government but may not give to the poor, carry on education, or teach religion outside of church. State publishing houses in turn cannot publish religious literature; schools cannot teach religion but must actively teach atheism; and the government has embarked on a campaign to discourage orthodox religious participation and aggressively promote atheism.[10]

So while the edifice of the church is retained, it is a hollow structure; the work of the people of God, which is the true church, is forbidden. Yet in officially promoting atheism, the state is offering its own substitute religion to legitimate its own structure.[11]

Encroachment upon faith in the West is usually not as dramatic as it has been in modern totalitarian states. It begins in minor ways, such as a county zoning commission barring Bible studies in homes, suppers in church basements, or religious activities on public property. And even when it appears that the state is accommodating religious viewpoints, its action may well be a Trojan horse. Though my opinion is perhaps a minority one, I believe the much-debated issue of prayer in schools is a case in point.

Children or teachers who want to pray in schools should have the same rights of free expression and the same access to public facilities any other group has. But organized prayer, even if voluntary, is another matter. The issue is who does the organizing. If it is the school board, Caesar is being given a spiritual function; admittedly a small crack in the door, but a crack nonetheless. I for one don't want my grandchildren reciting prayers determined by government officials. And in actual practice they would be so watered down as to be of no effect except perhaps to water down my grandchildren's growing faith.

Whenever the state has presumed on God's role, whether in

ancient Rome or modern America, the first liberty, freedom of conscience, suffers.

On the other side of the coin, the church, whose principal function is to proclaim the Good News and witness the values of the Kingdom of God, must resist the tempting illusion that it can usher in that Kingdom through political means.[12] Jesus provided the best example for the church in His wilderness confrontation with Satan when the devil tempted Jesus to worship him and thus take dominion over the kingdoms of this world.

No small temptation. With that kind of power, Christ could enforce the Sermon on the Mount; love and justice could reign. He might have reasoned that if He didn't accept, someone else would. This rationalization is popular today, right up through the highest councils of government: compromise to stay in power because there you can do more for the common good.

And think of the popularity Jesus could have gained. After all, the people wanted a Messiah who would vanquish their oppressors. But Jesus understood His mission, and it could not be accomplished by taking over the kingdoms of the world in a political coup.

Yet the most consistent heresy of the church has been to succumb to the very temptation Christ explicitly denied. In the Middle Ages this produced bloody crusades and inquisitions; in modern times in has fostered a type of utopianism expressed in a stanza from one of William Blake's most famous poems:

> I will not cease from mental flight,
> Nor shall my sword sleep in my hand,
> Till we have built Jerusalem,
> In England's green and pleasant land."[13]

This century's social-gospel movement echoed Blake's senti-ments, dissolving Christian orthodoxy into a campaign to eliminate every social injustice through governmental means. Objectives became political and economic to the detriment of the spiritual. The reformers' well-intentioned efforts were shattered as social programs failed to produce the promised utopia, leaving observers to conclude, "Things are no better. Where is your God now?"

Utopianism is often articulated today in contemporary Chris-tian circles; it crosses political lines, from the liberation theologians to the New Right and to the mainline church leaders. As one bishop confided to Richard Neuhaus, "The mission of the church is to build the kingdom of God on earth, and the means of the mission is politics."[14]

Such preoccupation with the political diverts the church from its primary mission. This was evident in the comment of an Ameri-can lay missionary who described liberation theology as "a concern for man and the world as opposed to the concern of the traditional church for the salvation of man's soul."[15] All Christian political movements run this risk.

They run another risk too, particularly those on the political right where many want to impose Christian values on society by force of law. Some, such as those in the theonomist movement, even want to reinstate Old Testament civil codes, ignoring Christ's teaching in the parable of the wheat and the tares in which He warns that we live with both good (the wheat) and evil (the tares), and cannot root out the tares. Only God is able to do that and He will—when the Kingdom comes in its final glory.

It is on this point that the church most frequently has stum-bled in its understanding of the Kingdom of God. Oscar Cullman writes: "In the course of history the church has always assumed a false attitude toward the state when it has forgotten that the present time is already fulfillment, but not yet consummation."[16] Even if Christians advocating dominion gained power, they would be doomed to failure. As Martin Luther once wrote, "It is out of the question that there should be a Christian government even over one land...since the wicked always outnumber the good. Hence a man who would venture to govern...with the gospel would be like a shepherd who should place in one fold wolves, lions, eagles and sheep together and let them freely mingle."[17]

It was perhaps because he realized this truth—that the world cannot be ruled by spiritual structures and that the church has long abused power—that John Paul I at his inauguration in 1978 refused to be crowned with the papal tiara, the vestigial symbol of the claim to temporal power. John Paul II followed his example. These dramatic gestures renounced a centuries-old tradition that has contributed to the darkest moments for the church.

But while the church must avoid utopianism and diversion from its transcendent mission, it is not to ignore the political scene. To the contrary, as will be explored in later chapters, its members, who are also citizens of the world, have a duty, as Carl Henry puts it, "to work through civil authority for the advancement of justice and human good." They may provide "critical illumination, personal example and vocational leadership."[18] Wilberforce is a prime example. There are proper ways as well for the institutional church to provide society with its moral vision and hold government to moral account.[19]

Through the individual Christian's involvement in politics, as we will discuss later, the standards of civic righteousness can be influenced by the standards of righteousness of the Kingdom of

God. Such an influence is what theologians call common grace (as distinguished from God's special grace that offers citizenship in the Kingdom of God to all who desire admission). Common grace is God's provision for the welfare of all His created beings, both those who believe in Him and those who don't.

The critical dynamic in the church-state tension is separation of institutional authority. Religion and politics can't be separated—they inevitably overlap—but the institutions of church and state must preserve their separate and distinct roles. In this regard, the American experiment merits closer examination.

America is not the New Jerusalem or a "city upon a hill," though some of its founders harbored that vision. Nor are Americans God's chosen people. The Kingdom of God is universal, bound by neither race nor nation. But Abraham Lincoln used an interesting phrase; Americans, he said, were the "almost chosen people."[20] If there is any justification for that term—not theologically but historically—it is because in the hammering out of a new republic, the combination of wisdom, reason, and providence produced a church-state relationship that uniquely respected the differing roles of each.

The basis of this radical idea came from the partial convergence of at least two conflicting ideologies: confidence in the eighteenth-century Enlightenment belief that both public and private virtue were possible without religion; and a reaction against the excesses of the state church in Europe. The first view was held by the Deists among America's founders, while the second particularly motivated the avowed Christians among them.

These men and women believed that Christ had given the church its own structures and charter, and the state, ordained in God's providence for the maintenance of public order, was not to

tamper with it. The church was ordained principally for the conversion of men and women—conversion grounded in individual
conscience wrought by the supernatural work of a sovereign God
upon the soul. So the state could neither successfully establish nor
destroy the church, since it could not rule conscience nor transform people's hearts and souls.[21]

Thus two typically mortal enemies, the Enlightenment and
the Christian faith, found a patch of common ground on American soil. Both agreed (for different reasons) that the new
government should neither establish nor interfere with the
church.[22] It was this reasoning that led to the adoption of the First
Amendment, expressly to protect the individual's right to freedom
of conscience and expression, and to prevent the establishment of
a state church.

But contrary to the belief of many today, this separation of
church and state did not mean that America was to be a nation
free of religious influence. From the very beginning the American
Revolution itself was seen by many as a rebellion fueled by the
conviction that man is a creature of God, and his political life is
conditioned by that truth. As James Madison insisted, "This duty
[homage to the Creator] is precedent, both in order of time and
degree of obligation, to the claims of civil society. Before any man
can be considered as a member of civil society, he must be considered as a subject of the governor of the universe."[23] A nation
under God was no idle phrase.

Nor did the separation of church and state mean religion and
politics could be separated or religious values removed from the
public arena. For one's political life is an expression of values, and
religion, by definition, most profoundly influences values.[24]

The Founding Fathers were well aware that the form of limited government they were adopting could only succeed if there was an underlying consensus of values shared by the populace. I am always reminded of this when I visit the House of Representatives. A beautiful fresco on the upper walls of the chamber itself contains the portraits of history's great lawmakers. Standing at the speaker's desk and looking straight ahead over the main entrance, one's eyes meet the piercing eyes of the first figure in the series: Moses, the one who recorded the Law from the original Lawgiver.

John Adams eloquently acknowledged the understanding of our constitutional framers when in 1798 he wrote: "We have no government armed in power capable of contending with human passions unbridled by morality and religion...Our constitution was made only for a moral and religious people. It is wholly inadequate for the government of any other."[25]

Many of these original American visionaries believed that Christian citizens would actively bring their religious values to the public forum. George Washington faintly echoed Augustine when he asserted, "Of all the dispositions and habits which lead to a political prosperity, religion and morality are indispensable supports. In vain would that man claim that tribute of patriotism, who should labor to subvert these great pillars of human happiness."[26]

Thus, when laws were passed reflecting the consensus of Christian values in the land, no one panicked supposing that the Christian religion was being "established" or that a sectarian morality was being imposed on an unwilling people. The point of the First Amendment was that such convictions could only become the law of the land if a majority of citizens could be persuaded (without coercion), whether they shared the religious foundation or not, of the merits of a particular proposition.

Today's widespread relegation of religion to merely something people do only in the privacy of their homes or churches would have been unimaginable to the founders of the republic—even those who personally repudiated orthodox Christian faith. Though America has drifted far from the vision of its founders, this system continues to offer one of the world's most hopeful models in an otherwise contentious history of conflict.

The record of the centuries should not cause despair, however. Tension between church and state is inherent and inevitable. Indeed, it is perhaps the outworking of one of God's great mysteries, part of the dynamic by which He governs His universe. For from the constant tension—the chafing back and forth—a certain equilibrium is achieved.

To maintain this balance the church and the state must fulfill their respective roles. One cannot survive without the other; yet neither can do the work of the other. Both operate under God's rule, each in a different relationship to that rule.

Certainly one thing is clear. When they fail in their appointed tasks—that is, when the church fails to be the visible manifestation of the kingdom of God and the state fails to maintain justice and concord—civic order collapses. The consequences can be catastrophic.

THE SERPENT
IS DOOMED

ERWIN W. LUTZER

Erwin W. Lutzer
Senior Pastor of Moody Memorial Church
Author and conference speaker

There was a scuffle as the serpent thrashed about, his fangs upright, hissing at his opponent. As the loathsome beast lay gasping, it attempted to strike but could only nip the heel of the foot that stepped on its head. When the frenzy was over; the head of the serpent lay crushed, pounded into the hard dirt, its body throbbing with pain. While drops of its poison lay spent on the ground, the victor returned to heaven in triumph.

At last, Christ was here. Centuries earlier, God had said to the Serpent, "And I will put enmity between you and the woman, and between your seed and her seed; he shall bruise you on the head, and you shall bruise him on the heel" (Genesis 3:15). God had made good on His Word.

When Christ was born in Bethlehem, Satan's first strategy was to kill him. Wicked King Herod tried to carry out the diabolical deed. But Joseph and Mary took the baby to Egypt, and the plan was foiled.

If he could not kill Christ, he would seek to corrupt Him! But in the desert, Christ proved that He would not bow to satanic temptation. Try as he might, Satan could not convince Christ to take a shortcut in becoming the rightful ruler of the world. Not even Peter was able to pressure Christ into choosing life rather than death in Jerusalem. "Get thee behind me, Satan," Christ told him (Mark 8:33, KJV).

Once Satan saw that Christ was headed toward Jerusalem, he stopped trying to prevent the Cross and chose to become a key player in the drama. The reason for the switch of tactics is not difficult to understand. If Christ was going to the Cross, then the Serpent wanted the satisfaction of knowing that he had a part in it. His sadistic delight in seeing Christ hang helplessly between heaven and earth, though fleeting, was a temptation he could not resist. Yes, he knew his judgment would be greater; yes, he knew that the Cross would mean eventful defeat. But that was tomorrow. For today, he would inspire men to kill the Lord's Christ, no matter how illusory the victory.

THE CROSS, THE CONFLICT

How do we know that the Cross was a time of satanic conflict? First, Satan himself entered into Judas to betray Christ (John 13:27). Though we frequently read of demon possession in the New Testament, as the decisive conflict looms, Satan himself comes to do the dirty work. There was to be no mistake—Christ would be turned over to the political authorities of the day. Judas would be the human vehicle to do a satanic deed.

CAN [GOD] RECONCILE US AND STILL RETAIN HIS HOLY INTEGRITY?

Second, Christ conceded that this was the hour for evil to take over and do its work. After Judas betrayed Him, Christ told His disciples that they should not retaliate. Then, turning to the chief priest and officers, He said, "Have you come out with swords and clubs as against a robber? While I was with you daily in the temple, you did not lay hands on Me; but this hour and the power of darkness are yours" (Luke 22:52–53).

"For the moment you win!"

Christ was willing to go toe-to-toe with His enemy and in effect say, "Yes, you may humiliate Me. Yes, you will see Me crucified naked. Yes, you will gloat over My apparent weakness." For a brief moment the Serpent would be elated. But he would celebrate too soon. If time belonged to Satan, eternity would belong to God.

Third, Christ Himself saw the Cross as the decisive victory. "Now judgment is upon this world; now the ruler of this world shall be cast out. And I, if I be lifted up from the earth, will draw all men to Myself" (John 12:31–32). Even in His "weakness," Christ would be striking the telling blow to Satan on his turf. The "ruler of this world" would be defeated in the world he claims to rule.

We've often heard that Satan was judged at the Cross. We know that he was "cast out" on this decisive battle, the focal point of history. And yet we also know that God has allowed him to continue to wield extraordinary power in this world.

What does it mean to say that the Cross crushed the head of the Serpent? And how were we included in Christ's victory?

THE CROSS, THE CONTESTANTS

The Cross, incredibly enough, is about us.

The question to be settled is whether God can reconcile us to Himself and still retain His holy integrity. To put it briefly, the issue is this: do any of us have the right to belong to God forever despite the fact that we are members of a race that sided with Satan? Or, how can unholy people become the sons and daughters of a holy God?

There is a scene in the Old Testament that fits this dilemma exactly. Joshua, a high priest (no relation to Joshua the military commander), is pictured as standing before the Lord clothed in "filthy garments." No doubt he felt just as dirty within as he appeared to be without. Even righteous people feel sinful in the presence of God.

Then, as if Joshua's own sense of shame were not enough, we read that Satan was "standing at his right hand to accuse him." (For the whole story read Zechariah 3:1–7.) That's about all you need when you are overwhelmed with guilt and failure—the devil at your side to whisper in your ear how bad you really are! He who is more wicked than we could ever be is on hand to judge our wickedness!

But this story does paint an accurate picture of our predicament. The fact is, we also are "filthy"—a strong word, but one that is apt when we stand in God's presence. And Satan does accuse us, insisting that we have no right to belong to God. We can be thankful that God has a remedy for the moral distance that exists between us and Him. He says to us, just as he did to sinful Joshua, "See, I have taken your iniquity away from you and will clothe you with festal robes" (Zechariah 3:4).

Imagine a courtroom scene. God is judge, Satan is the accuser, and we stand in Joshua's shoes. The question arises: What can be done to help us pitiful sinners as we stand in God's presence? If something is to be done, God must do it. Unless He acquits us, and figuratively speaking gives us those clothes of righteousness, we would be cast aside. After all, Satan does have a point. We are sinners who don't deserve to be loved and accepted by God.

Take note that the conflict between God and Satan is always waged over us; we are the trophies. If we are believers in Christ, Satan knows he cannot have our souls, but he will try to destroy our fellowship with God. Satan will do all that He can to dispute God's plans and judgment. But God will always win the battle for those who are His.

Just how He won that battle for us is the subject of this chapter. Giving us "festal robes" so that we no longer need be under the Serpent's domain involved an ingenious plan. And Satan, our accuser, who talks when he should be silent, was struck dumb.

THE CROSS, THE COURTROOM

How I wish a video camera had been able to record the drama that took place in the spiritual world when Christ died on the Cross! A cosmic battle was being fought. The devil was there, God was there, and Christ was there—and so were we. Just read Paul's words, keeping in mind that we will explain the details in a moment.

> When you were dead in your transgressions and the uncircumcision of your flesh, He made you alive together with Him, having forgiven us all our transgressions, having canceled out the certificate of debt consisting of decrees against us and which was hostile to us; and He has taken it out of the way, having nailed it to the cross. When He had disarmed the rulers and authorities, He made a public display of them, having triumphed over them through Him. (Colossians 2:13–15)

To unravel this passage, we must turn again to a courtroom scene, describing the key players, pinpointing the issues, and reporting the outcome. All the while, we must remember that it is our eternity that hangs in the balance. Don't forget, this is about us.

The Accusation

For openers, we are sinners, both by nature and by choice. We have all felt the agitation of a troubled conscience. But the sins we can remember are only a small part of the sum total of our guilt before God. Paul wants us to feel the full weight of the charges against us, or at least to be reminded of how far-reaching they really are.

He describes God's law, which we have broken, as "the certificate of debt consisting of decrees against us and which was hostile to us" (Colossians 2:14). Whether we know it or not, God's commandments have a claim over us. We are not free to write our own rules for the simple reason that God has already written them. But these laws were "hostile" to us; before them we stand condemned. So these decrees had to be taken out of the way before fellowship with God was possible.

In the courts of Saul's day, if you were brought before a judge, there had to be a hearing where the accused would be interrogated to see whether there was enough evidence to warrant a trial (today, we are more sophisticated and call it a grand jury). Recall that when accusations were made against Christ, Pilate questioned Him to see whether he deserved a hearing. When he saw that the charges were false, he said to the multitude, "I have found no guilt in this man" (Luke 23:14). Nevertheless, Pilate's cowardice led him to submit to the cries of the mob.

In our case, God does not have to ask us questions to probe for clues of guilt or innocence. He knows much better than we the extent of our guilt. That is why Paul says that in the presence of God's law "every mouth [is] closed, and all the world [is] accountable to God" (Romans 3:19). So we stand in shameful silence. No words escape our lips.

The devil, our accuser, is not quite so controlled. He speaks and has much to say. I believe he still has access to heaven today and is angry when we stand whole and clean on this earth, enjoying the presence of God. He reminds God of His promise that "the soul who sins will die" (Ezekiel 18:4). As an accuser, he quite possibly approaches God with a list of our sins; he comes armed with reasons we should be cast away from the divine presence. Let us never forget that his accusation is just. God Himself has said that "the wages of sin is death" (Romans 6:23). This time, Satan speaks at least some truth.

Of course Satan does not tell God anything that the Almighty does not already know. In fact, God knows more about us than Satan could ever comprehend. The dispute is not whether we have committed sins or not. The matter at hand is not whether we are as bad as Satan says we are. Rather, the controversy is over what should be done about our predicament.

Satan says, "You should *damn* him!"

God says, "I will *save* him!"

Perhaps we should pause to remind ourselves that the charges against us are not only accurate but extensive. In God's court we do not have to steal to be considered a thief, do not have to commit adultery to be considered an adulterer, and do not have to fashion a god to be an idolater. All that we need to do is to fantasize, desiring to do these things. What is more, we not only sin, but we are actually sinners; that is, we are seen as being in a state of sin. Nothing is hidden.

Not surprisingly, Satan insists that if we are allowed into heaven, we will defile its courts. God, he says, could be accused of associating with men who are unclean. Indeed, both the reputation and the truthfulness of God would be questioned. After all, it was the Almighty Himself who proclaimed His holiness and warned that sin brings death.

Satan's accusation against us follows one of two directions. Objectively he accuses us before God, arguing that we are too sinful to be acquitted. Subjectively he preys on our conscience, trying to make us feel so guilty that we shy away from God's grace. He who lures us into sin turns to condemn us for doing his bidding. And if that doesn't work, he will reverse himself and make us feel so good about ourselves that we believe we do not need God's grace at all.

Satan's one objective is to keep us separated from fellowship with God. He wants us to be on our own, just as he is. On our own, with him at our side?

The Penalty

Satan insists, perhaps quite reasonably, that we should have the same judgment as he. After all, we also are tainted with sin and are also rebels. If the greatness of the sin is determined by the greatness of the One against whom it is committed, then, indeed, we are supremely guilty. Let us be judged along with the Serpent, since we have a drop of the Serpent's poison.

Satan knew that he could count on God to hold fast to His standard of righteousness. He who had served as the Almighty's primary representative was confident that if His Master did not waver in His high standards, mankind would be abandoned to hell. Yes, the evil one knew that God was loving, but he also knew that His love could neither override nor cancel His justice. There could be no exceptions, even for people who did the best they could in this life.

Satan thought it was unfair that men could be eternally saved while he was eternally damned. Satan's point, which seems reasonable enough, is that each being should pay for his own sin; that would be just. After all, that is what Satan had to do. Sin is sin. Justice is justice. And God is God.

The ingenious plan Satan could not foresee is that, in the case of humans, one human would die for other humans. Specifically, one infinite human would die for a group of finite ones. God would thus keep His promise that "the soul who sins will die" (Ezekiel 18:4)—but someone else would do the dying. The wages of sin would still be death, but someone else would die in our stead.

Liberal theologians have often criticized the biblical teaching that Christ died for sinners by saying that it would be immoral for God to punish an innocent person on behalf of a guilty one. The answer, however, is that Christ was not innocent. He was made sin for us: "He made Him who knew no sin to be sin on our behalf, that we might beome the righteousness of God in Him" (2 Corinthians 5:21). Christ was declared to be a sinner, although He had never sinned; and we were declared to be saints, although we are decidedly "unsaintly."

Yes, Christ was regarded as a sinner; He became legally guilty of all of our sins, from lying to genocide. He was deemed guilty of unimaginable crimes. Because His guilt and punishment was *real,* we have a *real* Savior who can save us from some very *real* sins.

When was Christ "made sin for us"? Not in the Garden of Gethsemane, although Christ suffered there in deep agony and sorrow. Not when the crown of thorns was placed on His brow and the blood flowed from His forehead to his chin and then dripped onto His chest. Only when Christ was on the Cross did the transaction take place. When He shed His blood and actually died, we were redeemed.

Let us not overlook this comment in the Book of Deuteronomy: "And if a man has committed a sin worthy of death, and he is put to death, and you hang him on a tree, his corpse shall not hang all night on the tree, but you shall surely bury him on the same day (for he who is hanged is accursed of God), so that you do not defile your land which the Lord your God gives you as an inheritance" (Deuteronomy 21:22–23). Christ had to be hung, crucified on the Cross, before He could be declared cursed of God in our behalf. The moment He was placed there, He drew upon Himself the wrath of God. Paul put it clearly. "Christ redeemed us from the curse of the Law, having become a curse for us—for it is written, 'Cursed is everyone who hangs on a tree'" (Galatians 3:13).

Only when the nails were put through His hands, only when the Cross was lifted up with His body hanging on it, only when He breathed His last could God's wrath, which was stored up against sin, be expended. God the Father could not look upon one who was so thoroughly accursed. This separation, this anger directed toward His beloved Son, caused the anguished cry, "My God, my God, why hast thou forsaken me?" (Matthew 27:46, KJV). Thus we have a Savior.

Let's look at this transaction through Paul's imagery. He says the decrees that were against us were "nailed...to the cross" (Colossians 2:14). In those days, when a criminal was hung on the cross, his crime had to be publicly proclaimed. The list of transgressions was written on a placard and nailed above the dying man. Recall that Pilate put a notice above Christ's head with the accusation, "JESUS THE NAZARENE, THE KING OF THE JEWS" (John 19:19). He wrote it in three languages Hebrew, Latin, and Greek (v. 20). He wanted everyone to see the crime Christ was accused of committing.

It is true, of course, that Christ was the king of the Jews; in this, Pilate's words and God's verdict agreed. Needless to say, however, this hardly deserved punishment. It was not a crime to speak the truth. Yes, Christ was the king of the Jews, but it was not for this that He was dying.

High above Pilate's words, there was a cosmic bulletin board on which our sins were listed. Though I wasn't born yet, the sins that I would commit two thousand years later were recorded there. The list included everything that Satan had said about us as well as other secret sins that were known but to God. Only the Almighty knows how long the list of accusations was; only He knows the extent of our sin and the severity of its penalty.

God, then, did not see Christ as dying for His own crimes; nor, for that matter, was Christ a victim of circumstances that got out of control. He was delivered by the "predetermined plan and foreknowledge of God" to redeem sinners (Acts 2:23). "But He was pierced through for our transgressions, He was crushed for our iniquities; the chastening for our well-being fell upon Him, and by His scourging we are healed...But the LORD was pleased to crush Him, putting Him to grief" (Isaiah 53:5, 10).

The penalty was just. And the penalty was fully paid.

The Verdict

God has pronounced us *forgiven!*

With the accusations against us taken out of the way, God

maintained His holiness and yet acquitted us. As Paul says, He has "forgiven us all our transgressions" (Colossians 2:13).

God made no secret of Christ's success. Ancient Rome had a victory parade when the soldiers returned from a successful battle. The victors not only marched with the captive prisoners of war in tow, but they displayed the goods captured in battle. The Romans gloated in victory, choosing the main highway to enter the city. Just so, Satan's defeat was a public event, not to us, but to the entire spirit world. To quote Paul again, "When He had disarmed the rulers and authorities, He made a public display of them [the rulers and authorities]" (Colossians 2:15).

Satan was thus publicly disarmed. In Greek, the word translated *disarmed* means "stripped of weapons." Christ stripped him of his presumptuous insistence that he could continue to fight against Him and be successful. Satan was shorn of his pride and his supposed right to hold us as subjects in his kingdom. Though our mouths were closed in the presence of Satan's accusations, his mouth is now closed in the presence of our acquittal.

The victory of Christ does not mean, however, that Satan can no longer fight against us. Think of it this way. God stripped King Saul of his title as king even though he was still allowed to harass King David for ten long years. Although the forces who war against us had their authority removed, they continue to fight. They prefer to live in denial rather than face the humiliation of defeat.

In *Satan Cast Out*, Frederick S. Leahy says that it is only from our standpoint that there seems to be a gap between the victory of Christ over Satan and the final disposal of the defeated foe. He reminds us that lightning and thunder take place at the same time, but we see the light before we hear the rumble. He writes:

In objective reality, these are virtually one, but from our standpoint, owing to the fact that light travels more quickly than sound, there is usually a time-lag between seeing the flash and hearing the thunder: With God, the victory and the judgment are all in the cross.[1]

We can say that we have seen the lightning, but we have not yet heard the crash of his fall. With God, there is no such gap; He regards the judgment and sentence as already complete. "Now the ruler of this world shall be cast out" (John 12:31, italics added). And again, "The ruler of this world *has been judged*" (John 16:11, italics added).

THE SPECIFICS OF CHRIST'S VICTORY

How, then, did Christ defeat Satan at the Cross?

Christ Reconciled Sinners to God—Permanently

Christ satisfied our debt so completely and justly that we who believe in Christ no longer owe God any righteousness. Since the penalty for sin was not life but death, Christ had to die and in so doing reconciled us to God forever.

Consider that phrase once more: "having forgiven...all our transgressions" (Colossians 2:13). How many of your sins were future when Christ died two thousand years ago? Obviously, all of them, since not a one of us had yet been born. God anticipated our sin and included it in Christ's death. Christ not only died for the sins of the Old Testament saints but also for those who would become saints in the future. As the song goes, "I was on His mind when He died."

Now let me take the logic a step further. What about the sins you will still commit tomorrow and the day after? The answer, of course, is that for those who believe on Christ, even those sins have already been forgiven. It must be so, for if when we received Christ we were only forgiven for our past sins, we could not be sure of our future salvation. The reason we know we will go to heaven when we die is that God has forgiven our sins—past, present, and future.

Of course, we must still confess our sins, not to maintain our status as sons but to maintain fellowship with our Father. Legally, all of our sins have been taken away. We can rejoice in the security of our salvation because we have been acquitted, completely and forever.

The author of Hebrews put it this way: "But He, having offered one sacrifice for sins for all time, sat down at the right hand of God...For by one offering He has perfected for all time those who are sanctified" (Hebrews 10:12, 14).

One High Priest, *one* offering, *one* act of justification whereby we are declared righteous. As He did with Joshua, God gives us clothes to wear that cover our sins:

Jesus, Thy blood and righteousness
My beauty art; my glorious dress;
'Midst flaming worlds in these arrayed,
With joy shall I lift up my head.

For those who do not accept Christ as their substitute, Satan's original indictment stands. But for those who believe, we have been taken out from Satan's kingdom and have been transferred into the kingdom of Christ.

Christ Silenced Satan

Satan's mouth was shut. His whimpering accusations stopped. The Judge of all the earth had declared us righteous—who was

Satan to say otherwise? Can the failed god contradict the Lord of heaven and earth? To free men, Christ had to win a victory over the accuser of men. He who tried to keep men and women in bondage had to be exposed, his power destroyed, and his prisoners set free.

In biblical times, if a placard of the man's crimes was put on his prison cell, it was returned to him when he had served his punishment. When he was allowed to take it home, it was no longer an indictment but a trophy! Across it was written *Tetelesti* that is, "Paid in full."

If a neighbor asked him whether he was legally free, he could show him the document. The debt of justice had been served. There was nothing left to pay. Significantly, Christ's last words from the Cross were *tetelesti,* translated "It is finished" (John 19:30). Our debt was "paid in full."

Jesus paid it all,
All to Him I owe;
Sin had left a crimson stain,
He washed it white as snow.

If God were still to expect a payment from us after Christ paid our debt, there would be unrighteousness with God. Our debt was paid so fully that no further payment will ever be necessary. This is why we can say, "There is therefore now no condemnation to them which are in Christ Jesus."

Recently a woman wrote to tell me about her bad marriage. She ended by saying, "I've given up trying to please God. If I can't please my father and my husband, I will never please Him."

How would you have answered? I wrote back, "I have some

good news for you: You do not have to try to please God; God is already more pleased with Christ than He could ever be with you or me, even if we have several good days in a row! If you trust Christ, God is as pleased with you as He is with His blessed Son whom He dearly loves."

Of course this must be balanced with the equally true challenge of Scripture that we should strive to please God (1 Corinthians 9:24-27; 2 Timothy 2:4). But we cannot please Him until we know that He is already pleased with us. Only when we know that we are His beloved children in "whom He is well-pleased" are we at peace, able to live desiring to please God in our daily experience.

On particularly difficult days I have prayed, "O, God, today please do not look on me at all, look only upon Your Son and see me as complete in Him." I know that God also wants me to become like His Son in everyday living, but I will never please God as Christ has; therefore, I delight to rest in His work on my behalf.

I often receive letters from people who believe that they have committed the "unpardonable sin." Now of course, there is an "unpardonable sin"; it is the sin of unbelief, the hardness of heart that often accompanies those who have heard the gospel message but are determined to reject it.

But no Christian can commit the "unpardonable sin." Those who have transferred their trust to Christ have had their sins pardoned. Christ has canceled all of our transgressions. He knew us long before we were born; He knew the evil we would do; and He covered it all.

When Satan accuses us, we must show him our canceled certificate and read aloud, "Paid in full." We must say to him,

"Begone! for it is written, 'Who will bring a charge against God's elect? God is the one who justifies; who is the one who condemns? Christ Jesus is He who died, yes, rather who was raised, who is at the right hand of God, who also intercedes for us'" (Romans 8:33–34).

Our attorney, Christ, has pleaded our case, and God has accepted His plea. And when God speaks, the universe listens.

Christ Proved He Had the Power of Life

Satan can only kill; he cannot make alive.

In order for God to prove His complete superiority, He had to raise Christ up from the dead so that there would never be any dispute over who was Lord and King. For this reason, the resurrection of Christ is a necessary part of the gospel message (1 Corinthians 15:3–5). Death, which is itself the consequence of sin, was fearful, but Christ conquered it for us. "Since then the children share in flesh and blood, He Himself likewise also partook of the same, that through death He might render powerless him who had the power of death, that is, the devil; and might deliver those who through fear of death were subject to slavery all their lives" (Hebrews 2:14).

Of course Satan never had the power to determine when a person would die. Such matters belong to the risen Christ, who won the honor of possessing the keys of death and Hades. Satan does, however, hold the tyranny of death over our heads; and in the case of the unconverted, death slams the door of opportunity to believe in Christ.

A butterfly was observed inside a windowpane, fluttering in great fright. It was pursued by a sparrow who kept pecking at the butterfly, eager to devour it. What the butterfly could not see was the pane of glass that separated the two of them. The butterfly did not realize that he was as safe next to the sparrow as he would have been had he flown to the South Pole. Just so, the invisible Christ comes to shield us from Satan's power. The Serpent can hiss and taunt, but he cannot devour. We have a different King; we serve in a different kingdom.

Christ came to deliver us from the fear of life and the fear of death. His resurrection proved that He was stronger than the grave. And when He ascended into heaven, He opened its gates for all who would believe on Him.

Christ Opened the Gates of Heaven

Not all Bible scholars agree, but I believe that those who died in faith in the Old Testament went to Hades, and not until the Ascension of Christ were they taken up to heaven. Paul wrote that when Christ ascended, "He led captive a host of captives, and He gave gifts to men" (Ephesians 4:8). Perhaps that means that those who were in the righteous compartment of Hades were taken to heaven at that time.

Regardless of this we can be sure: Christ's death opened heaven to those who are His children. To the thief on the Cross He could say, "Today you shall be with Me in Paradise" (Luke 23:43). There is now a direct route to heaven, opened by One who Himself has entered. Death no longer is our enemy but a friend that takes us to God.

When a little girl was asked why she was not afraid to walk through the cemetery, she answered, "Because my home is on the other side." Once a bee has stung its victim, it cannot strike a second time. It can only annoy and terrify, but its sting has been exhausted. Christ took the sting out of death and assures us that "to be absent from the body [is to be] present with the Lord" (2 Corinthians 5:8, KJV).

When Stephen was stoned, he could already see Christ waiting for his arrival. Indeed, the Son of God stood to welcome His faithful child home. The gates of heaven await all who believe.

Christ Exalted Us Above the Angelic Realm

Would you change places with the angel Gabriel? Think before you answer. We might be tempted to envy a being that had such beauty and power. We just might think that he is a cut above us. True, we can never approach the strength and beauty of an angel. We cannot even imagine what it would be like to fly through the universe doing assignments for God.

> *We will have an honor*
> *beyond what he enjoyed.*

And yet, we shall be above the angels. No angel can ever be called a brother of Christ. It follows that no angel can ever be an "heir of Christ." For a little time Christ became lower than the angels, for no angel has ever died. For a little time we are lower than the angels, but that too will change (Hebrews 2:5–13).

Again we must return to God's eternal perspective. God has taken us from the pit to walk in the palace "that the manifold wisdom of God might now [since the Cross] be made known through the church to the rulers and the authorities in the heavenly places" (Ephesians 3:10). Put simply, God wanted to show off His grace. So He took sinners who had fallen so low and exalted them so high!

We are to judge the world;

We are to judge angels;

We are to be heirs of God and joint heirs of Christ.

No wonder Satan is furious. The fact that we will have an honor beyond what he enjoyed before his fall from grace is more than his envious nature can tolerate. Think of all that he had already given up. He could no longer be a prophet who could speak for God. He could no longer be a priest who would direct worship to God. He could no longer be a messenger bearing messages for God. He who wished to be like God has ended up the most unlike Him. In short, it was all loss and no gain.

Today he is out on bail. He is allowed to roam until his final judgment. The sentence to the lake of fire has only been postponed. The verdict has already been read. We have seen the lightning. The thunder is on its way.

My wife and I have visited the Wartburg Castle in Germany, where Martin Luther spent ten months in hiding. There, in a small room, perhaps no bigger than fifteen feet square, he anguished, often feeling the attacks of Satan. Tradition says that in that room he threw his inkwell at the devil. Perhaps his comment in the *Table Talks* gives a different interpretation of the event, when he said, "I fought the devil with ink." He may have meant that he fought the devil by translating the New Testament into German.

We can be quite sure that his attacks from Satan were many. Yet the strength and safety of the Wartburg and other fortresses gave him the inspiration to write his famous hymn, "A Mighty Fortress Is Our God." One of the stanzas reads:

And though this world, with devils filled,
Should threaten to undo us,
We will not fear, for God hath willed
His truth to triumph through us.
The prince of darkness grim—
We tremble not for him;
His rage we can endure,
For lo! his doom is sure,
One little word shall fell him.

And what is that "little word"? It is the six-letter word *Christ.* Christ, properly understood, can "fell him."

The Cross proved it.

If we ask why Satan has not already been consigned to the pit, the answer is that God is using him to complete the divine plan. The Serpent is actually God's servant. He served before he fell and he is serving even now. He has a different motivation, and the conditions are far worse than they once were, but he is a servant nonetheless.

How Satan Causes You to Sin

JOHN PIPER

John Piper
Pastor of Bethlehem Baptist Church
Author and conference speaker

Two Great Enemies of Our Soul

The two great enemies of our soul are sin and Satan. And sin is the worst enemy, because the only way that Satan can destroy us is by getting us to sin. God may give him leash enough to rough us up, the way he did Job, or even to kill us, the way he did the saints in Smyrna (Revelation 2:10); but Satan cannot condemn us or rob us of eternal life. The only way he can do us ultimate harm is by influencing us to sin.

Which is exactly what he aims to do. All his other shenanigans—like sickness and lost visas and spooky sounds and green apparitions and various intimidations—all these things cannot do us ultimate harm, unless they lead us to sin. So Satan's main business is to advocate, promote, assist, titillate and confirm our bent to sinning. We see this in Ephesians 2:1–2. Paul says, "You were dead in your trespasses and sins, in which you formerly walked...*according* to the prince of the power of the air." Sinning "accords" with Satan's power in the world. When he brings about moral evil, it is through sin. When we sin, we move in his sphere, and come into accord with him. When we sin, we "give place to the devil" (Ephesians 4:27, KJV).

The only thing that will condemn us at the judgment day is unforgiven sin—not sickness or afflictions or persecutions or intimidations or apparitions or nightmares. Satan knows this. Therefore his great focus is not primarily on how to scare Christians with weird phenomena (though there's plenty of that), but on how to corrupt Christians with worthless fads and evil thoughts.

WHAT SATAN KNOWS ABOUT THE SPRING OF SIN

But Satan also knows something else—far better, I think, than many Christians know it—namely, that all sin comes from failing to live by faith in future grace (see Romans 14:23). Which means that the number one aim of Satan is the destruction of faith. Faith in future grace is the spring of radical righteousness. It's the root of love and all Christ-exalting living. And its absence is the root of all sin. Satan knows this. Therefore he aims all his efforts, one way or the other, at the prevention or destruction of faith in future grace.

Satan's Jagged Sieve

You can see this in the way Jesus prayed for Simon Peter just before Peter's great temptation. He said, "Simon, Simon, behold, Satan has demanded permission to sift you like wheat; but I have prayed for you, that your faith may not fail; and you, when once you have turned again, strengthen your brothers" (Luke 22:31–32). Satan's aim was to sift Simon Peter. What does that mean? Jesus gives us the clue by saying, "I have prayed *that your faith not fail."* This must mean that what Satan wanted to do was to sift the faith out of Peter. Satan has a sieve with a jagged mesh designed to sift the faith out of Christians. That's his main goal.

Paul implies the same thing in 1 Thessalonians 3:5. He is concerned about the new church he had just started in Thessalonica. So he sends Timothy to see how they are doing. Timothy comes back with a good report, and Paul writes this letter to explain what his deepest concern really was: "When I could endure it no longer, I also sent to find out *about your faith,* for fear that *the tempter* might have tempted you, and our labor should be in vain." Paul's greatest concern was that Satan would have attacked their faith and ruined the work he had begun.

Similarly, when Peter writes to the churches of Asia Minor, he warns that Satan is always prowling around trying to "devour someone." Then Peter adds, "Resist him, firm in your faith" (1 Peter 5:9). This implies that Satan wants to catch us at a time when our faith is not firm, when it is vulnerable. It makes sense that the very thing Satan wants to destroy would also be the means of our resisting his efforts. That's why Peter says, "Resist him, firm *in your faith."* It is also why Paul says that the "shield of faith" can "extinguish all the flaming missiles of the evil one" (Ephesians 6:16). The way to thwart the devil is to strengthen the very thing he is trying most to destroy.

Without Faith in Future Grace We Will Only Sin

All true virtue comes from faith in future grace; and all sin comes from lack of faith in future grace. Faith works through love—faith in future grace is the spring of all true obedience and holiness and love. The flip side of this truth—that failing to have faith in future grace, that is, failing to be satisfied with all that God is for us in Jesus—is the root of all sin. Satan knows this; and it shapes his whole strategy of how to get people to sin.

It's important that we see this as clearly as he does, so that it can affect our counterstrategy. All the sinful states of our hearts are owing to unbelief in God's super-abounding future grace. All our sin comes from failing to be satisfied with all that God is for us in Jesus. Misplaced shame, anxiety, despondency, covetousness, lust, bitterness, impatience, pride—these are all sprouts from the root of unbelief in the promises of God. Let me illustrate from a familiar text that seems to trace all sin back to a surprising source, the love of money.

The Heart That Loves Money

Paul said in 1 Timothy 6:10, "The love of money is the *root of all evils*" (literal translation). What did he mean? He couldn't have meant that money is always in your mind when you sin. A lot of sin happens when we are not thinking about money. My suggestion is this: he meant that all the evils in the world come from a certain kind of heart, namely, the kind of heart that loves money.

Now what does it mean to love money? It doesn't mean to admire the green paper or the copper coins or the silver shekels. To know what it means to love money, you have to ask, What is money? I would answer that question like this: money is simply a symbol that stands for human resources. Money stands for what you can get from man instead of God. God deals in the currency of grace, not money: "Ho! Every one who thirsts, come to the waters; and you who have *no money* come, buy and eat." (Isaiah 55:1). Money is the currency of *human* resources.

So the heart that loves money is a heart that pins its hopes, and pursues its pleasures, and puts its trust in what human resources can offer. So the *love* of money is virtually the same as *faith* in money—belief (trust, confidence, assurance) that money will meet your needs and make you happy. Love of money is the alternative to faith in future grace. It is faith in future human resources. Therefore the love of money, or trust in money, is the underside of unbelief in the promises of God. Jesus said in Matthew 6:24, "No one can serve two masters…You cannot serve God and mammon." You can't trust in God and in money at the same time. Belief in one is unbelief in the other. A heart that loves money—banks on money for happiness—is not banking on the future grace of God for satisfaction.

Whatever Is Not from Faith Is Sin

So when Paul says that the love of money is the root of all evils, he implies that unbelief in the promises of God is the taproot of every sinful attitude in our heart. He said it even more plainly in Romans 14:23, "whatever is not from faith is sin." The absence of faith gives rise only to sinful motives and acts. This may sound extreme. But it is simply a clear expression of Paul's radical God-centeredness. What does not come *from* satisfaction in God, and *through* the guidance of God, and *for* the glory of God, is Godless—it is sin. And no matter how philanthropic or esteemed or costly it may appear among men, it is deficient in the main thing; love for the glory of God.

There are numerous pointers in the Bible that putting our trust in anything but God causes sin. For example, there seems to be a connection between trusting money and the enticement into sin in Job's defense of his integrity: "If I have put my *confidence in gold, and called fine gold my trust…*and my heart became secretly enticed, and my hand threw a kiss from my mouth, that too would have been an iniquity calling for judgment, for I would have denied God above" (Job 31:24, 27–28). Confidence in gold and trust in fine gold leads to denying God and committing sin. Similarly, when the Proverb says, "He who *trusts in his riches* will fall" (Proverbs 11:28), it probably means that he will come to ruin through a life of sin.

Isaiah warns those who trust in human military resources that this false trust will lead to evil and sin, and eventually to destruction. "Woe to those who go down to Egypt for help, and *rely on horses,* and *trust in chariots*...But they do not look to the Holy One of Israel, nor seek the LORD!" (Isaiah 31:1). Then he describes the Lord's judgment in response to this reliance on human resources and rejection of future grace. Surprisingly he says that the judgment is upon evil and iniquity—the outcroppings of faith in human fortune. "[God] will arise against the house of *evildoers,* and against the help of the *workers of iniquity*" (Isaiah 31:2). The point is that unbelief in the future grace of God produced "evildoers" and "workers of iniquity" (see Hosea 10:13–14).

Trusting the Gift of Goodness, Not the Giver

One of the saddest instances of false hope occurs when people trust in what God has worked in them instead of trusting God himself. For example, God says, "When I say to the righteous he will surely live, and he so *trusts in his righteousness that he commits iniquity,* none of his righteous deeds will be remembered" (Ezekiel 33:13). It is possible to trust in your own goodness in such a way that it produces iniquity. Any trust, except in God, brings about sin. "You *trusted in your beauty* and played the harlot because of your fame" (Ezekiel 16:15). God had made Israel beautiful. But when she became satisfied with her beauty, instead of her Beautifier, the result was harlotries.

The point I am pressing is the one that Satan knows and uses: where faith in God fails, sin follows. For Satan, this means that the focus of his work is the subversion of faith. This fits with his fundamental character. Jesus said, "Whenever [Satan] speaks a lie, he speaks from his own nature; for he is a liar, and the father of lies" (John 8:44). This is his primary means of subverting faith. Faith stands or falls on the truth that the future with God is more satisfying than the one promised by sin. Where this truth is embraced and God is cherished above all, the power of sin is broken. The power of sin is the power of deceit. Sin has power through promising a false future. In temptation sin comes to us and says: "The future with God on his narrow way is hard and unhappy; but the way I promise is pleasant and satisfying." The power of sin is in the power of this lie.

Satan's main strategy is to use a thousand devious ways to make this lie look appealing and persuasive. The beginning of all our misery came from Satan's first great success on the earth. It was not by means of scaring or harassing or possessing Adam and Eve. It was by deceiving them. And the deception was just this: God cannot be trusted to meet your needs and satisfy you. The serpent says only two things. One is a question that suggests God is stingy, "Has God said, 'You shall not eat from any tree of the garden'?" The other utterance is a murderous half-truth, "You surely shall not die!" (Genesis 3:1, 4).

In his penetrating study of the Pentateuch John Sailhamer sums up the scene like this:

The snake speaks only twice, but that is enough to offset the balance of trust and obedience between the man and the woman and their Creator. The centerpiece of the story is the question of the knowledge of the "good." The snake implied by his questions that God was keeping this knowledge *from* the man and the woman (Genesis 3:5), while the sense of the narratives in the first two chapters has been that God was keeping this knowledge *for* the man and the woman (e.g. 1:4, 10, 12, 18, 21, 25, 31; 2:18). In other words, the snake's statements were a direct challenge to the central theme of the narrative of chapters 1 and 2; God will provide the "good" for human beings if they will only trust him and obey him.[1]

Satan began by calling God's goodness into question and that has been his primary strategy ever since. His aim is to subvert trust by influencing us to believe that the promise of sin is more satisfying than the promise of God.

Promise against Promise

The only actions Satan really cares about are future actions. The sins of the past are gone. He cannot change them. He can only deepen them, by influencing our future responses to them, or add to them, with more future sins. All sins that can be committed are future sins. If Satan is going to bring us into sinful states of mind and into sinful actions, he will have to use promises. This is what he did with Adam and Eve. This is what he does with us. He holds out alternative promises of God-neglecting pleasure.

To do this he must blind the mind of unbelievers and distort the spiritual perception of believers. "The god of this world has blinded the minds of the unbelieving, that they might not see the light of the gospel of the glory of Christ, who is the image of God" (2 Corinthians 4:4). Satan's only hope of success is to hide the truth and beauty of Christ from the mind of man. It is the glory of Christ that compels the heart to embrace Him in the promises of future grace. Satan makes every effort to obscure this compelling glory, so that we will not be satisfied with all that God is for us in Jesus.

What this means for living by faith in future grace is not only that it is a lifelong battle, but that it is specifically a battle *against sin* (which is the only condemning instrument Satan has), and a battle *for faith* (which Satan wants most to destroy).

Don't Listen
to Your Loins

JAY CARTY

Jay Carty
Director of Yes Ministries
Author and speaker

THE CONSEQUENCES OF SEXUAL SIN

Beth was a homemaker with two kids, a high school daughter and a junior high son. Her husband, Randy, was a middle-management corporate climber. They went to church together as a family but weren't deeply involved. Actually he went because she wanted them all to go. It was quality time with the kids and they enjoyed eating out together afterwards, so he went.

As a couple their mutual interests had grown in different directions over the years. She took the kids to the athletic and school events. Randy usually worked late. There was an athletic club close to the office. That's where he got his workouts. Beth played tennis in the mornings with her friends. They called themselves "the girls."

One morning, after playing only one set, the game broke up early. Two of the ladies had forgotten a prior commitment. The third left. Beth had a soda and relaxed for a moment at a table.

That was when Jack was looking for a partner for mixed doubles.

Jack was a business acquaintance of Randy's and was exceptionally nice and "terribly good looking." She played and had a great time. But she politely refused to have a drink with the group after the game.

Two days later she found herself sitting at the same table at almost the same time, hoping to play some more mixed doubles. She had thought a great deal about the wonderful time she'd had. Although it didn't happen on Wednesday, to her inward delight it did happen on Friday, and yes, she did have the postgame drink with the group. It seemed right to do so. Jack was considerate beyond words and unbelievably attentive to her needs. It was like he knew what she was thinking ahead of time. He made her feel like a queen, not a housewife.

Staying for a drink was Beth's second compromise. Her first was sitting at the table on Wednesday—hoping. She had failed to set her boundaries in concrete ahead of time.

And yes, two weeks later she slept with Jack. She hadn't meant to. It just kind of happened. And now, here she is trying to figure out what to do.

Jack wants to leave his wife for Beth. Beth is attracted to Jack, but he is already on his third marriage and that's scary. Besides, she loves Randy, even though the thrill is gone. And what about the kids? What happens when Randy finds out? Where does God fit into all of this?

Stay and be unhappy. Leave and be unhappy. Face the kids and be unhappy. When Randy finds out she'll be real unhappy, and so will he. Is it possible to be away from God and be happy? She didn't think so. What a mess, and it's only a matter of time until her house of cards comes tumbling down. There will be consequences to Beth's immorality.

God prizes sexual purity more than any other act of obedience. That makes destroying it satan's number one priority. And
since slavery to sex is so captivating, the discipline from God necessary to alter the problem of mastery to sexual enslavement must
be greater than any other. It all makes for some very interesting
consequences. Beth will find that out soon enough.

SATAN HATES VIRGINS AND PURITY

We live in enemy territory and sometimes satan is not very subtle.
For example, whose name is the only proper name used as a
swear word? Sure...Jesus Christ. When is the last time you heard
someone in a fit of temper say, "Oh, Jay Carty!" Never. Have you
ever heard anyone miss a putt playing golf and scream, "Chuck
Swindoll" or "James Dobson"? Me neither. How about "Ronald
Reagan" when the car won't start? Nope! Listen, Jesus has the
most popular name going. No other name comes close. You'll
hear it in locker rooms, on the job, and in the movies. It's called
profanity. The Bible calls it using the Lord's name in vain.

Why is that precious name used as a swear word? And why
does God say not to do it? He knew what satan would do with
that name—attempt to pervert it. Even an old jock like me can
figure that out.

In the Church of Satan, they do all the opposites of Christianity; the goal is to corrupt Christ. The cross is turned upside
down and the arms are broken into a peace sign. They worship a
goat instead of the Lamb. And their number one act of worship is
the virgin sacrifice. As a matter of fact, you cannot get married in
that church unless you've had intercourse.

Satan's desire is to brutalize the virgin birth of Jesus Christ.

Therefore, I believe *the number one goal of the devil is to steal your virginity. His next priority is to move you into immorality.* That's what he did with Beth.

Since satan hates God, he wants you to do what God doesn't want you to do. What's important to God is important to the devil…but satan's reason is to pervert and debauch. Why does the enemy want the virginity of our children and why does he want the rest of us to fall into immorality? Because moral purity is so important to God. To understand its importance, it's necessary to understand something about out sin nature and why God hates sexual sin.

THE IMPORTANCE OF THE VIRGIN BIRTH

When my daughter was a toddler, we had a low-profile stereo that had sliding doors in its top. Kim thought it was fun to slide the doors back and reach in; there was some good stuff in there to play with. There was a switch that clicked, a wheel to spin, and an arm to yank on.

In our household a "Daddy no-no" was an automatic, no questions asked, hand slap. One day when Kim had her hand in the stereo, I said, "Kim, that's a Daddy no-no," and I slapped her hand.

Kim screamed but thrust her hand right back into the stereo. I took out her little hand and whapped it a second whap. She pulled the same routine. After screaming she thrust her hand back into the stereo. I'm going to make a long story short, but this is absolutely true. I whacked the hand twenty times, and twenty times she put it back into the stereo.

On the twenty-first whack Kim's whole disposition changed. Her whole demeanor altered. She thrust her face toward my face, glared, and defiantly thrust her hand back into the stereo while continuing to state at me. If she could have talked, she would have said, "Bite the wall, Dad! Hang it in your ear, Pop! I'm gonna do what I wanna do, because I wanna do it!"

I couldn't believe it. I was at war with a nine-month-old kid. I'm big, tall, ugly and I have a deep voice. Listen, I'm intimidating. I can be a scary guy, but that little nine-month-old kid wasn't afraid.

Again I took the little hand out of the stereo. By the way, Kim's hand was big, swollen, hot, and red by then. It looked sore—so I whacked it. She glared, started to thrust her hand back into the stereo, stopped, pondered, folded her arms, exhaled through her nose, turned and made her way to the other side of the room. It was over but it had been quite a battle.

Here's my point: where did she get that? I know, from me, right? You bet. *You and I were born with a sin nature and we got it from our dad.*

The Bible says, "Behold, I was brought forth in iniquity, and in sin my mother conceived me" (Psalm 51:5). Augustine thought the verse was referring to the sexual act of intercourse. He thought sex was sin. But that's not the meaning at all. The Bible was referring to the transfer of the father's sin nature to the child.

Our sin nature is transmitted through the male. That's why Jesus had to be born of a virgin, otherwise he would have received the sin nature of his dad. If that had happened he would have had to die for his own sins and wouldn't have qualified to die for ours. In that light, the virgin birth becomes a critical doctrine. And now you can begin to grasp why our enemy concentrates so much time and effort on perverting virginity.

GOD HATES IT THE MOST

While it's true that satan hates sexual purity more than any of God's other mandates, it is also true that God hates sexual sin more than any other sin and considers it to be unique among all the possible sins we can commit. The result is a principle:

> The consequences for involvement in sexual sin will be the most traumatic and severe God has to offer.

God's methods of dealing with immorality in the past proves my point. He has dished out consequences for it in ways he has never disciplined any other sin. This is illustrated in Luke 17:26:

> And just as it happened in the days of Noah, so it shall be also in the days of the Son of Man.

The phrase "the days of the Son of Man" refers to when the Lord will return. I call it the day of the great "too-doo." You don't know what a "too-doo" is so I guess I'd better tell you.

Have you ever sat in your bathroom, looked over at the paper holder, and realized that there is no tissue? All that's left is a little cardboard cylinder. Have you ever taken that little cardboard cylinder, put it to your lips, and used it for a trumpet..."too-doo"? Have you ever done that? I thought so. All right, have you ever used it for a telescope? Me too. Aren't we fun?

Well, just before our Lord returns there's going to be a very loud shout (YAHOO) and then you'll hear the greatest trumpet blast you've ever heard "TOO-DOO!" Listen, when you hear those two sounds get ready to leave the planet because we are jetting out of here. There won't be any floating up through the ceiling, saying, "good-bye, good-bye." The Bible says in the twinkling of an eye we'll be caught up into the sky.

"As it was in the days of Noah"; that's the way it will be when we're caught up in the air with the Lord. So how was it in the days of Noah? Let's read on.

> They were eating, they were drinking, they were marrying, they were being given in marriage, until the day that Noah entered the ark, and the flood came and destroyed them all. (Luke 17:27)

They were carrying on business as usual. But what kind of business was it? Genesis 6:5 tells us they were doing only evil continually. We don't know what kind of evil was actually being done, so let's read on.

> It was the same as happened in the days of Lot: they were eating, they were drinking, they were buying, they were selling, they were planting, they were building; but on the day that Lot went out from Sodom it rained fire and brimstone from heaven and destroyed them all. (Luke 17:28–29)

Where did Lot live? That's right, Sodom and Gomorrah. They, too, were carrying on business as usual. But what kind of business was it? In Jude 1:7 it tells us they were involved in gross immorality and were chasing after strange flesh.

Do you remember the story about the angels who went to rescue Lot? Oh, how that man loved the night life in Sodom. He didn't want to leave until morning. So the angels, who looked like men, decided to sleep in the city park. Lot nixed that idea. The angels weren't quite sure why Lot was so emphatic, but they agreed to sleep at Lot's house. They found out in the middle of the night. The men of the town were homosexuals and came to Lot's house to rape his guests.

It was the last straw before God destroyed the city, all except for one family...Lot's.

> It will be just the same on the day that the Son of Man is revealed. (Luke 17:30)

What was the last straw in the days of Lot before God destroyed everything except for one family? Sexual sin. What was the last straw in the days of Noah before God destroyed everything except for Noah's family? Sexual sin! And what will be the last straw in those final days just before our Lord comes back and destroys it all except for one family, his church? Sexual sin! And how is it today? Sexually gross. We've got our Sodom in Las Vegas and our Gomorrah in San Francisco. It's almost time for God's "too-doo" to make its sound.

What's the point? In the Old Testament there is only one other thing for which God destroyed so utterly and completely—idol worship. But do you remember what he called it? Spiritual adultery. That's heavy stuff and a principle is wrapped up inside.

> Sexual sin is the negative standard by which the severity of all other sin is measured.

Like it or not, immorality is a big deal with God. And woe to the person who doesn't get the message.

Remember the concept of mastery? The stronger the slavery, the stronger the discipline necessary to change the behavior. Therefore the consequences for violating God's sexual mandates will be tougher than for any other sin you can commit. It's best to do what's right because it pleases God, but sometimes a little fear isn't bad.

Christian leaders are dropping like flies to adultery and sexual promiscuity. People of stature and status toward whom we look for leadership are failing to stay pure. The result is their ministries are taken from them. Sure, in Christ they are forgiven. Repentance restores their relationship with the Holy Spirit, but their impact on the Body of Christ is seldom the same again. There is very little room for leaders to stray sexually. God does not want the dominoes to fall.

You may be saying, "Jay, I want to hear about the love of God. Don't preach the fear of God to me."

Listen carefully, I spend half my time on the road and there's been an occasion or two when it's just been a solid dose of the fear of God that's kept my nose clean. I have even gotten to the point of being willing to disobey God, but I was afraid of the consequences. I knew the outcome would be too severe. A time of physical pleasure followed by a few seconds of zing can never substitute for destroying a family, ruining a ministry, and causing the dominoes who look to you to stumble and fall. Besides, the resulting footholds can cause so many problems.

There is a reason God hates sexual sin more than any other sin. Sexual sin messes with the mechanism of creation, and that's where eternal souls are created.

AN INTERNAL VIOLATION

God considers every other sin external in nature. Only sexual sin is considered an internal violation of the dwelling place of the Holy Spirit. God considers immorality as different from all other sins…it's distinct and unique. He said so:

> Every other sin that a man [woman] commits is outside the body, but the immoral man [woman] sins against his [her] own body. Or do you not know that your body is a temple of the Holy Spirit who is in you, whom you have from God, and that you are not your own? For you have been bought with a price: therefore glorify God in your body. (1 Corinthians 6:18b–20)

Immorality is put in a different category. I'm not sure why, but let me give you a guess from the Book of Hesitations.

How long will the souls of my two children last? Forever! Whether they end up in heaven or hell, their souls will last forever. My wife and I made something that is going to last forever. Not even the angelic host can do that or make that claim. Just us. And since making eternal souls is such an unusual privilege, as best as I can tell, God doesn't want the mechanism of creation violated until it is in the sanctity of the marriage bed, especially when the sins of the father are visited upon the children (Exodus 34:7). God considers sex to be holy ground and it's not to be violated. I guess that's why satan is always so quick to make footholds out of our foul-ups.

If God hates sexual sin so much, and if he considers it to be so unique, there must be more to immorality than meets the eye. There is.

THERE'S MORE TO IMMORALITY
THAN MEETS THE EYE

To understand what happens during immoral intercourse, it's necessary to understand the word *cleave*. Cleaving is not putting two pieces of paper together and separating those two pieces of paper or putting two boards together and separating those two boards. It's like mixing flour and water. What do you get? Paste. Glue. Something different from that with which you started. The flour and water have intertwined. They have cleaved and can't be separated into two parts again, at least not in the same way they existed before bringing them together.

Paul was referring to the word *cleave* when he used the phrase "the two will become one flesh" in 1 Corinthians 6:15–17:

> Do you not know that your bodies are members of Christ? Shall I then take away the members of Christ and make them members of a harlot? May it never be! Or do you not know that the one who joins himself to a harlot is one body with her? For He says, "THE TWO WILL BECOME ONE FLESH." But the one who joins himself to the Lord is one spirit with Him.

Paul said that intercourse intertwines the participants. In a sense, they become one body, and when separated they will never again be the same. That's good in the sanctity of the marriage bed since sexual intimacy between couples is facilitated in ways no other act can accomplish. But outside of God's blessing the consequences are detrimental and can be lifelong.

The world says sex is just physical. Hopefully you enjoyed it, and when it's over, that's it. But sex is more than physical bonding.

You are body, soul, and spirit (1 Thessalonians 5:23). Emotions are either a part of the soul or the spirit (probably the soul). That makes it impossible to cleave and not have an emotional intertwining. When the intertwining occurs out of wedlock, a scar is always produced. I call this scar a monster. In Amnon's case it was a monster of bitterness produced through intercourse.

YOU CAN STOP

Amnon, David's son, had a half sister named Tamar. Tamar was a "fox." We're talking the cutest—and she was a virgin. Virgins were a rare commodity in those days too. Amnon wanted her desperately, and sexually fantasized about her every day to the point of making himself sick. He got "ouchies" in his side.

> Absalom...had a beautiful sister whose name was Tamar, and Amnon...[lusted after] her. And Amnon was so frustrated because of his sister Tamar that he made himself ill, for she was a virgin. (2 Samuel 13:1–2).

Let me put what happened to Amnon in modern day terms. The parents of a high school girl go out for the evening so she calls her boyfriend over to watch a little television. There are no éclairs in her refrigerator, she's not in a double-minded condition, she just wants to spend part of an evening with her boyfriend.

He shows up, they turn on the tube, and watch *Cosby*. Part way through, the young couple is enjoying a little kissy-face and huggy-bod, but that's it. It's no big deal...to her way of thinking anyhow. However, mastery has overcome him.

If you are a young man, I'm going to blow your cover in this particular situation. Our stallion repeats a standard line for guys at times like that. He says, "Don't stop me now, you can't stop me now, because if you stop me now it's going to hurt me. So don't stop me now, you've got to keep going because we've gone too far. We've got to go all the way because if you stop me now it will hurt me."

The young lady thinks about what he said, but as she ponders, headlights from her folks' car flash through the living room window as they pull into the driveway, home unexpectedly early.

Here's a question for you. Could the guy stop or not? You bet he could! What was the situation when her folks walked into the house? Was everything cool? You bet your sweet begonias. Were there any problems? Are you kidding? Nobody suspected a thing.

Could the guy stop? Of course. Did he think he could stop? Nope, at least not until his reason for stopping was greater than his desire to press on. And when he got home that night the worst thing that might have happened would be a little twinge in his side. He might have had to rest for a little while with one knee bent before falling asleep, but that's all that would have happened. Really! That's it.

Gals, I hope you don't get yourselves into situations like that, but if a guy ever lays that line on you just say, "Oh no you don't. Go on home and take a cold shower. At the worst, all you'll have is a little ouchy in your side, but it won't be any big deal. I'll see you later."

If you work at an office with a mover type, draw your boundaries early. Don't let familiarity change your standards. If you're in high school, decide what behaviors are pleasing to God and don't change them. If you're in a boring marriage don't allow your situation to alter God's standards for you. Don't cave in. Compromise is a cruncher, as we will see. That's why your rules have to be established at the beginning of a relationship and reemphasized in your mind at the beginning of each evening. There is a principle involved:

In the heat of passion there are no rules.

Sexual activity captivates. It consumes. In passion and panic all rules go out the window. But remember the polar bear alert principle: *When your imagination comes in conflict with your will, your imagination will usually prevail.* You most often end up doing a variation of that which you think about the most. That's what happened to Amnon.

TAMAR'S COMPROMISES

Amnon refuses to stop thinking about getting Tamar into bed, so he goes to his friend and asks him for advice. His buddy tells him, "Call your old man on the phone and tell him you're sick and that you need Tamar to come over and make some hot cakes for you so you will feel better."

Amnon thinks that's a great idea so he calls his dad and tells him he's got a bad case of the punies. When David arrives at his son's bachelor pad, Amnon is faking the flu, and in verse 6 says something like, "Gee, Dad, I'm really sick. Would you send Tamar over here to care for me? I need some help. Some hot cakes would sure make me feel better, and nobody makes hot cakes better than Tamar."

Being a rather typical out-of-touch, out-to-lunch dad, David falls for it and sends for Tamar to make some hot cakes for Amnon. Do you think I'm kidding about the hot cakes? I'm not. Read verse six:

> So Amnon lay down and pretended to be ill; when the king came to see him, Amnon said to the king, "Please let my sister Tamar come and make me a couple of cakes in my sight, that I may eat from her hand." (2 Samuel 13:6)

See, hot cakes. You thought I was kidding. Not me. No sir!

So Tamar went to her brother's house and he was lying down. She took the Aunt Jemima pancake mix and made that boy some flapjacks (vs. 8).

Then Amnon painted a pained look on his face, held his arm to his brow, and faked agony as he spoke, "Tamar, I can't stand the noise from all the servants. All day long they've been making a clamor. Dismiss them for me will you? Send them away. I can't stand it any more. Thanks so much" (vs. 9).

He sneaked a peek and added, "No, you stay please, I'll need some help with the cakes."

Why did she stay? Have you ever thought about that? No? I think I know.

She had no intention of going to bed with him, although it was kind of fun to be there...in his pad. And after all, it was her dad who sent her there. I think the biggest reason she stayed was that Amnon made her feel desirable. She didn't always feel that way. But feelings can get you into big trouble.

Most of us have self-image problems these days. That's why we are so susceptible to anyone who makes us feel attractive. Her back went "zing, zong, zing"; she got little goose bumps on her arms, and it kinda' felt nice to feel desirable. So she stayed. She compromised just a little. Tamar didn't realize that goose bumps and hot cakes don't mix.

Groaning, Amnon spoke again, "Oh, I think it's the Hong Kong flu. I'm so weak Tamar, I can't even move my hand to my mouth. Would you bring the food in here and feed me please? No joke, I'm wasted. I'm really sick." He took another peek to see if she was falling for it (vs. 10). She was.

If he'd called her on the phone and said "Tamar, would you

come over here and go to bed with me," she would have laughed in his face. But because of some feelings, she's in his bedroom, alone with him, and he's in bed. That's the situation after just two compromises.

She didn't intend what is about to happen to happen. He's the snake. He's the toad. I'm not blaming Tamar. He's premeditated this thing; he's the bad guy. But Tamar had fulfilled her obligation to her spiritual authority, and she should have gotten out of there after she made the cakes. She could have, but the goose bumps got her. Now it's too late. Because Amnon grabs her and says, "Come, lie with me, my sister" (vs 11).

Tamar screams, "No, don't do this terrible thing," and she meant it. There is no double-mindedness; she wanted out of there. But he was stronger, pulled her to himself, and raped her (vs. 14).

I don't want the ladies to hear me putting any blame on Tamar (so many women have been abused along the way), but in this case she'd had the opportunity to leave. But because Tamar liked the way she felt, she stayed a little longer than she should have. Goose bumps can be expensive. *Compromise will get you into big trouble.* Amnon staged his plan and Tamar made the necessary compromises. The cost of goose bumps is high. Tamar found that out…too late. It was too late for Amnon too. Neither would be the same.

AMNON'S MONSTER

Sexual relationships outside of marriage rarely last, and attitudes change after having premarital sex. That's the way it was for Amnon after he raped Tamar. He got a scar…a monster of bitterness.

> Then Amnon hated her with a very great hatred; for the hatred with which he hated her was greater than the [lust] with

which he had [lusted after] her. And Amnon said to her, "Get up, go away!...throw this woman out of my presence, and lock the door behind her." (2 Samuel 13:15, 17)

What's Amnon's attitude toward Tamar after he's had her? "Get up, go away, get out of my sight; you make me sick; I hate your guts," is the essence of what he said. That's pretty strong talk. Amnon is not the same. His feelings have changed. And it happened after he'd had sex. Bitterness was the outcome of his sexual encounter.

A physical relationship alone will not keep and hold a person. A man or a woman who tries to hang on to a member of the opposite sex with his or her body will end up being despised and usually cast aside. Don't miss this message. It happens all the time. It's so easy to mistake lust for love. *Sure, I'll put out for him because he loves me,* the young high school girl thinks. But after he gets what he wants the mystique is gone. He hates her for being easy and casts her aside. The next day at school she has to face him— knowing he knows her most intimate secrets and that his friends know also. She, too, ends up bitter.

The principle these high schoolers experienced applies to all ages, including folks who are currently married.

Did you have sex with your spouse prior to the sanctity of marriage? Was physical attraction the basis of your relationship? If you answered yes to either question, have you ever wondered about the subtle hostility that exists between you as a couple? The reason is the principle found in 2 Samuel 13:

Bitterness is the outcome of premarital sexual encounters.

If you got married on the basis of a physical relationship, the chances are that you got divorced. The thrill lasted nine to fourteen months. Figure six months of discouragement, a few months to decide, several months of processing the papers, and you found yourself divorced within two to three years. But if you happen to still be together, if the mandate not to divorce has prevailed in your life, you've had some tough times over the years, haven't you?

Why does bitterness exist between you? Where did it come from? Could it be a foothold of oppression from your immoral past? Probably! If so, it's a monster of bitterness.

MIND MONSTERS

Monsters take form in ways other than bitterness. Those who have been promiscuous have visual images of past encounters unexpectedly pop into their mind—and sometimes at most inopportune times. It's like taking a trip through a grotesque art gallery, only you never know when you're going. That image is a monster, and the trip is a consequence of sin. Satan's agent is the tour guide.

If you ever used pictures to stimulate yourself sexually, you occasionally have flashbacks. Older men actually have flashbacks to the pictures of their youth. Women flash to the romance they'd once hoped for. Why? Because you cannot look at a person with lust in your heart without committing adultery or fornication (Matthew 5:28). Lusting after pictures creates an emotional intertwining—a visual monster, a scar. People who are hooked on pornography know the reality of mind monsters; scars are part of the consequences of sexual sin.

IT'S NEVER THE SAME AFTERWARDS

That's the way it is with illicit sex of any kind. Things are never the same afterward. Scott found that out the hard way.

Four high school guys were out looking for a little fun—two

seniors, a junior, and Scott, who was a sophomore and the starting quarterback for the team.[1] The older three decided to get some beer. "The evening will be more fun with half a case to 'sip' on," they said.

Scott had never had a beer but he didn't want to look like a sissy in the eyes of his new friends, so he had a few. *It's no big deal,* he thought. Then the driver pulled a little bottle of pills out of his coat, took one, and passed them on. He wanted to have more fun than a beer could produce. Each of the guys took one, including Scott. Although he had never done uppers before, he wanted to be one of the guys. One little compromise. What will it hurt? *My folks will never find out.*

Someone lit up and passed a joint. Scott took a hit. *What could happen? Is it really any worse than alcohol?*

Looking for something a bit more exciting they decided to cruise lovers' lane. Seeing a lonely car with a two-headed body in the front seat, the three upperclassmen silently crawled up to the vehicle. Scott was lagging behind a bit. The three jumped to their feet and yelled, trying to scare the occupants. Then they began bouncing the car. When the driver got out and approached one of them, the other two jumped him and hit him and hit him and hit him, just for fun, until he was helpless on the ground.

And then just for fun they put a bag over the girl's head and took turns. First the two seniors, then the junior, and then they called for Scott.

It seemed like the thing to do. All the guys had done it. He did want to be accepted. Being high provided a good excuse.

But as he finished, the girl, who had been motionless and whimpering, began to flail and fight. As she did the bag came off her head, and her eyes met Scott's eyes.

The girl he had just raped was his sister.

Compromise had taken its escalating toll and things would never be the same. Scott would be changed. Certainly his sister would be marred. The sister's boyfriend lost an eye from the beating; he would never be the same. I assume the three older guys now have a prison record, and they must be very different too.

I don't know what happened to Scott or his sister. I never saw a follow-up article in the paper, but certainly their looks and glances at each other would be forever different. Compromise caused it. Intercourse had sealed it. God's most intimate act had been violated, and relationships would forever be altered.

Scott's example is a violent one. So was Amnon and Tamar's. Although, Beth, Randy and Jack's example wasn't violent, they'll all be different. And so will the girl who put out for the guy who said he loved her. The reason?

When two unmarried people agree to have sex together,
when it's over they will never be the same.

Like gravity, it's one of God's rules.

Even though things will never be the same, there is a cure. There is a way to fix it. Not all of it, of course; you understand that you cannot undo a pregnancy, reestablish virginity, or get rid of AIDS. And deep emotional scars always leave a mark. But you can fix it—in God's eyes—and you can remove the footholds of the enemy. There is that kind of a cure, if you want it.

New Age
or
Old Lie?

KERRY D. MCROBERTS

Kerry D. McRoberts
Senior Pastor of Sumner Assembly of God Church
Teacher and author

A NEW AGE?

"Love what you are. Love the god that you are. Embrace the wind, and the willow, and the water, for it is the creation of your importance, and be at peace," says Ramtha, a 35,000-year-old warrior spirit which speaks through an attractive, lithe blonde from Yelm, Washington.[1] J. Z. Knight is known as a channeler for Ramtha, who once conquered the mythical kingdom of occult lore, Atlantis, and has now returned to the earthly plane to give spiritual guidance to literally thousands of people in America seeking entrance into a New Age. "The Ram" (as Ramtha is affectionately called), whose clientele includes actresses Shirley MacLaine and Linda Evans, predicts that the New Age will dawn in the year 2000.

Ramtha is only one among a myriad of "spirit guides" which are preparing the consciousness of individuals to enter into an age of universal enlightenment. "You need answers," says a harsh guttural voice through the clench-fisted, entranced channeler. "I am here to answer you."[2]

The controversial claims of Ramtha and a host of others (human and nonhuman!) who predict a coming New Age of planetary paradise for the inhabitants of earth was the focus of an open forum I recently participated in at Seattle Pacific University. Eight panel members, four representing evangelical Christianity and four representing New Age thought, individually responded to the primary issue of the evening, what is the New Age movement?

Responses to this question were varied: "it is a mystical, mind-altering experience...it is contrary to a Judeo-Christian worldview." A New Ager countered, "The New Age movement says that the source of God is the source of love and the source of God is within you;...this was Jesus' message." Another advocate of the New Age added, "The New Age is an age where new perceptions enable us to explore the unknown frontiers of our universe." A representative of evangelical Christianity contentiously replied, "For the first time in history there is a viable movement, the New Age Movement, that truly meets all the scriptural requirements for the Antichrist." "The New Age," retorted a somewhat indignant New Ager, "is typified by the individual's search to understand his own relationship to the God-force...the Christ within." The sincere commitment of the New Age to planetary survival was pleaded for by yet another "Aquarian conspirator." "The New Age is one of the most creative movements in the last part of the twentieth century...The attempt of the New Age...is to understand and be energized to meet the crises that are facing us today."

The diversity of the New Age has been analogized by one writer to the "proverbial elephant discovered independently by three blind men: one came upon his leg, and likened him as a tree; another got hold of his trunk and likened him to a hose; the third stumbled upon his tail and insisted he was like a rope."[3] This illustrates an invaluable point: when critiquing the New Age, we need to be aware that the consensus of a part may not be true of the whole.

The New Age is not simply another new cult, but an emerging worldview, a new way of thinking that is being subtly introduced to multitudes in Western civilization. This new way of thinking promises renewed hope to those disillusioned with former inadequate worldviews such as atheistic humanism. Through a change of consciousness (transformation in New Age terminology), the New Age seeks to bring about radical changes within the world community that will deliver the earth from its present sociopolitical ills.

The New Age is an extremely large, loosely structured network of organizations and individuals. The New Age weds the humanism of the West with the spirituality of Eastern occult mysticism. The union of these two unlikely bedfellows inflates former concepts of human potential in the West to unlimited proportions, generating a belief in the deification of man.

Several cults emphasizing a mystical experience (e.g., Transcendental Meditation, Church Universal and Triumphant, the Divine Light Mission, Scientology, Eckankar) subscribe to the New Age worldview. Various organizations and cults that are a part of the "human potential movement" also share this worldview. Familiar groups included here are est (Erhard Seminars Training, also referred to as Forum), Lifespring, Silva Mind Control, the Esalen Institute, and Summit Workshops. A significant number (though not all) of the holistic health centers in America also promote the New Age way of thinking. Individual followers of gurus (Baba Ram Dass, Sai Baba, Da Free John, etc.), agnostics, atheists, theologically liberal "Christians," and secularists in general all have representation in the ranks of New Age ideology.

Although there is a wide range of beliefs and emphases among groups and individuals that come under the collective banner of the New Age movement, certain basic assumptions are true of the whole. The edifice of New Age thought rests upon five distinctive philosophical pillars.

1. REALITY IS A "SEAMLESS GARMENT"

New Age thinking embraces the concept that everything in existence is one essential reality. The universe is perceived as a "seamless garment" without distinctions; all that is, is one reality.

Monism is another name for a "seamless," undifferentiated universe. Monism is a concept of Vedic Hinduism. *Monos* (Greek) means single; and therefore, ultimate reality is a single, organic whole without independent parts. Only reality wears the seamless garment, everything else is naked illusion.

Although the New Age embraces monism, it does not believe, as classic Vedic Hinduism, that the world is illusory or maya. The New Age is more of "a Western expression of monism."[4] Holding to its Western heritage, the New Age is world affirming. In other words, the external world is really there. It is not an illusion. The New Age has a paradoxical view of reality. Objects, events, and persons maintain a distinctiveness, and yet they are interdependent with the whole, a part of one flowing reality. As the offspring of two convergent worldviews, the New Age movement has characteristics of both parents.

Eastern monism suffers from grave epistemological (in philosophy, the grounds for knowledge) uncertainty. Monism is fatalistic in its view of the need to reject personality in order to attain to one's spiritual awareness (enlightenment). This results in an inescapable tension between the logic of what it teaches and the logic of who and what man really is. Eastern monism, therefore, fails to provide a sufficient spiritual option for Western man, who is faced with the dehumanizing influences of the failing worldview of atheistic humanism.

Atheistic humanism views man as the product of primordial, nonintelligent mass that by mere chance alone evolved to a human state of existence. Therefore, man is nothing more than a cosmic accident who has no inherent purpose. No matter how sublime our descriptions of man, this view ultimately strips man of any intrinsic self-worth. Since New Age man envisions himself on the threshold of a golden era, he must stretch his imagination beyond national boundaries to embrace Eastern monism and Western humanism as legitimate means of saving humanity from apocalyptic catastrophe.

2. God Wears the "Seamless Garment"

The belief that God is all in all, or that all that exists is an extension of God's essence, is pantheism. Apart from God, there is no true reality. Pantheism imbues the material universe with consciousness. Therefore, according to New Age thinking, matter is not dead, as in the thinking of the naturalist; instead, an impersonal force or consciousness is the essence of all reality. The "Force" of Star Wars fits into this type of metaphysical mode.

G. K. Chesterton poignantly observed that, "when a man ceases to believe in God, he does not believe in nothing. He believes in anything." Rather than a step of evolutionary progress, pantheism is a regression into pagan idolatry. Pantheism is the attitude into which the human mind will automatically fall when left to itself. Pantheism is what man says about God, instead of what God says about man. It is therefore not surprising that we, as sinful humans, find pantheism so congenial.

Ludwig Wittgenstein correctly stated (*Tractatus Logico-Philosophicus*): "If there is any value that does have value, it must lie outside the whole sphere of what happens and is the case...Ethics is transcendental." Pantheism, however, fails to provide an unchanging, transcendent point of reference for ethical decisions. If all that exists is one undifferentiated whole, then categories of good and evil are ultimately abandoned. Men are left with the inability to distinguish right from wrong in this kind of universe.

Men quite obviously are unable to live this way. Men must make ethical distinctions between good and evil, right and wrong. Norman Geisler observes that "In order to discover if a man really believes it is good to be just, do not look at the way he acts toward others; rather, look at the way he reacts when others do something to him."[5] Pantheism is self-defeating with regard to practical human experience.

3. MAN WEARS THE "SEAMLESS GARMENT"

It follows from pantheism that if God is all and all is God, then man, as a part of the "all," must be inherently god.

In the late sixties, during my undergraduate days at the University of Oregon, a question concerning ultimate reality was circulating around campus: "How are you going to recognize God when you get to heaven?" The reply: "By the big G on his sweatshirt."

The New Age, however, boldly declares that man really wears the sweatshirt with the big G. "Each of us," claims David Spangler, "is a dynamic process of God revealing himself."[6] Singer John Denver, a graduate of Erhard Seminars Training (Forum), enthusiastically agreed, "I can do anything. One of these days, I'll be so complete I won't be a human, I'll be a god."[7]

Beginning with evolutionary presuppositions as an explanation for the material existence of the universe, the New Age man sees himself at the peak of his evolutionary cycle. The birth of a mystical humanism is viewed as the result of an evolutionary metamorphosis wherein the New Age man has attained to godhood. New Age man, attired in his "sweatshirt," fearlessly kicks open the door of the occult, announcing his unqualified divinity.

Occult philosophy is the flip side of secular humanism. The occult, like humanism, stresses human potential through its exalted view of man as the source of all meaning in the universe. The occult, however, inflates human potential to cosmic dimensions and thereby deifies humanity. Occult philosophy defines God in terms of being created in the image of man. The occult phenomenon in America is the logical conclusion to a worldview that insists upon the absolute autonomy of man.

The Pseudo-Scientific Terminology of the Occult

Because of the use of scientific or pseudo-scientific labels, occult practices (i.e., yoga, visualization, spiritism, witchcraft, etc.) within the New Age go unnoticed. The deceptive packaging of the New Age grows out of a deliberate design of the occult to adapt itself to the prevailing cultural environment. Transcendental Meditation's venerated guru, Maharishi Mahesh Yogi, explains:

If the message is to be carried from generation to generation, it should be placed on the mass tendency of each generation...Therefore, basically, the teaching...should be based on that phase of life which at a particular time is guiding the destiny of mass consciousness...Thus the proper plan for the emancipation of all mankind, generation after generation, lies in...finding various ways and means for its propagation according to the consciousness of the times.[8]

The Maharishi is saying that the religious goals of his movement should not be presented in terms that are popular and acceptable to the majority of people. In chameleonlike fashion, the occult adapts its terminology to the vernacular of the social milieu it is attempting to influence; yet the meaning behind the artificial term is quite different from what people initially conceive.

Whenever...religion dominates the mass consciousness, Transcendental...meditation should be taught in terms of religion. Whenever metaphysical thinking dominates...[it] should be taught in metaphysical terms, openly aiming at the fulfillment of the current metaphysical thought. Whenever...politics dominates...[it] should be taught in terms of and from the platform of politics, aiming at bringing fulfillment to the political aspirations of the generation.[9]

The psycho-occult philosophy of the human potential movement is wrapped in scientific and therapeutic terminology. The saffron robes, shaved heads, and incense are replaced with three-piece suits, pseudo-scientific technology, and an emphasis on human potential.

The "Inner Truth" of the Occult

Inherent within the nature of the occult is the concept of an "inner truth" (the real truth known only to occult initiates) and an "outer truth" (the attractive, yet misleading face presented to the public). The successful penetration of the New Age into Western culture is due, in large part, to the deceptive design of a gap between an "inner truth" and an "outer truth." The vibrantly positive facade of the New Age acts as "sheep's clothing" for the spiritual delusion of the occult.

4. COSMIC CONSCIOUSNESS

Ultimate reality is a "seamless garment." God wears the "seamless garment." To the Western mindset, such a spiritual orientation appears rather insipid for its lack of diversity. What seems to be the problem? Ignorance. Timothy Leary of sixties infamy puts it this way:

> Our favorite concepts are standing in the way of a flood tide two billion years building up. The verbal dam is collapsing. Head for the hills or prepare your intellectual craft to flow with the current.[10]

We need to abandon the psychological limitations of Western thought and turn East. Man needs a change of consciousness, a mystical experience, to be made aware that he is really wearing the sweatshirt with the big G on the front, argues the New Age.

"Mystical states," says William James, "seem to those who experience them to be states of knowledge. They are insights into depths of truth unplumbed by the discursive intellect."[11] New Age author Marilyn Ferguson goes beyond a mere description of cosmic consciousness to the experience itself:

Loss of ego boundaries and the sudden identification with all of life (a melting into the universe); lights; altered color perception; thrills; electrical sensations; sense of expanding like a bubble or bounding upward; banishment of force, particularly fear of death; soaring sound; wind; feeling of being separated from physical self; bliss; sharp awareness of patterns; a sense of liberation; a blending of the senses (synesthesia), as when colors are heard and sights produce an auditory sensation; an oceanic feeling; a belief that one has awakened; that the experience is the only reality and that ordinary consciousness is but its poor shadow; and a sense of transcending time and space.[12]

Direct mystical states are the norm in the New Age. Propositional revelation (such as the Bible) is considered to be a barrier to spiritual awareness. Experience is the final authority. Methodology is de-emphasized. Therefore, numerous mystical-inducing methods are practiced by adherents of the New Age movement in order to attain cosmic consciousness. Techniques include Eastern meditation, yoga, martial arts, visualization, guided imagery, hypnosis, biofeedback, body therapies (rolfing, bioenergetics, kinesiology), seminar training (Erhard Seminar Training, Silva Mind Control, Foundation for Mind Research, Arica Institute), sensitivity groups, and many others.

In the New Age, the expanded consciousness of man is believed to be the most powerful acting force on the physical plane. The energies required in the ethereal counterpart to bring in the New Age are occultly under the control of human consciousness. The reordering of reality is limited to man's own state of mind, for the "New Age is consciousness first, form later."[13]

> Man must learn to build that culture through his atunement to the ideas of New Age, to externalize its characteristics from within his own creative consciousness. In this he will find his new glory and his fulfillment as a builder of a new heaven and a new earth.[14]

As the New Age man attunes his consciousness with the consciousness of ultimate reality, the idea of the New Age will materialize on earth.

Chris Griscom is a channeler from New Mexico. To her, the idealism of the New Age means, "We are the stars of our own movie...We are writing the script at all times."[15] In his book, *The Center of the Cyclone,* John Lilly is exuberant about reaching "+3," the highest state of consciousness:

> We are creating energy, matter and life at the interface between the void and all known creation. We are facing into the known universe, creating it, filling it...I am "one of the boys in the engine room pumping creation from the void in the known universe; from the unknown to the known I am pumping."[16]

For sociologist George Leonard, altered states of consciousness have brought him to the realization that "I am the universe."[17] In the New Age, the search for the higher self is united with the search for ultimate reality.

Channeling

Mafu is a "spirit guide" like Ramtha. Mafu is channeled by Penny Torres of Southern California. Mafu informs his audience that he has passed through four dimensions and 1908 years to bring his enlightening news to the inhabitants of earth: "I am an enlightened entity and I come to you from the Brotherhood of light."[18] Mafu claims that former President Ronald Reagan discussed a better day for the people of earth with "peoples of the inner earth." These "people" supposedly gain access to the Oval Office through secret polar tunnels![19]

Jach Pursel, a former insurance adjuster, is the channel for Lazaris. Lazaris, speaking with a British accent and a slight lisp, describes himself as "the consummate friend." The round, bearded Pursel sits on a simple platform in front of 400 people at Los Angeles's Hilton Hotel for a weekend seminar. Among Lazaris's guests is actress Sharon Gless, the feisty blonde detective of *Cagney and Lacy.* Gless sobs along with several others as Lazaris's comforting tones guide the crowd into the metaphysical wonderland of the New Age magic kingdom. The wounded psyches of those in attendance are placed in the hands of their trusted therapist, Lazaris. Soon it is time to leave the ethereal fantasyland and return to the physical plane. The reentry is made easier by Lazaris's assurances that, "You are now healed mentally; your old patterns can now be said no to."[20]

Kevin Ryerson is a colorful channeler. Ryerson is unique among New Age channelers in that he is a medium for five spirit entities, not just one. Among the disembodied residents of Ryerson's corporeal habitat are "John," an Essene scholar from the first century A.D., and an Irish pickpocket from the Elizabethan era known as "Tom MacPherson." Ryerson's fascination with the paranormal goes back to his childhood: "When all other kids were putting together model airplanes, I was studying ESP and Zener cards."[21] Influenced by Edgar Cayce (Cayce, who died in 1945, was a famous psychic known for his diagnosis of medical problems while in a trance), Ryerson is working with Dr. William Kautz of the Center for Applied Intuition in San Francisco in an effort to bring resolution to scientific mysteries.

Perhaps weekend seminars with average price tags of between $250 to $400 or private sessions priced at $90–$150 an hour are a little steep for many people. There are a number of cut-rate personal channelers available for those who either can't or just don't want to afford the more costly vintages of metaphysical insights served by Ramtha, Mafu, Lazaris, or John.

Harvey Huggins is a retired logger who lives in Oregon. For the meager price of a can of Copenhagen smokeless tobacco, Huggins will turn over his vocal cords to Wishpoosh, the beaver warrior-god of the Chinook Indians. The price of admission is worth it just to see how Huggins comes into contact with his entity. Huggins plunges his head into a bucket of water for a few minutes. As the old logger emerges and shakes the water from his beard, Wishpoosh is ready to share his metaphysical quips with the adventuresome.

If Nebraska is more convenient to the seeker of low-budget cosmic wisdom, then Cyril Jones is available. Jones channels the crass MacDoogie, a Scottish Highlander and warrior-accountant who lived in 23 B.C. MacDoogie hasn't changed in all these centuries of time; he'll tell you anything you want to know for a fifth of Glenlivet.

Roger Dodger is from Maine. Ramjet must find himself in comfortable surroundings living inside of Roger in Maine, for he is also from the high country—Tibet to be exact. Ramjet was a Shao Lin warrior-monk who lived around A.D. 900. You would think that a consultation with such an impressive figure as Ram-jet would cost at least as much as Ramtha. Not so! Roger Dodger owns a gas station in Pidwick, Maine, and the insightful consultations of Ramjet, the "one who lubricates the Wheel of Karma" are available to all customers. Just come in and fill 'er up!

Are these entities real? Are their channels for real? There are at least three possible responses to these questions. First of all, the entities are a part of the channeler's higher consciousness, and the message is sincere. Second, the entity is an actual spiritual being; and in the third case, the channeler is a fraud, feigning possession for the purpose of financial gain.

When interpreting messages "from the other side," their moral-theological content must be judged. The messages of the channelers are generally amoral, self-centered, paganistic affirmations of man's sinlessness and inherent godhood. Brooks Alexander further comments that "The thrust of most spirit messages is to deny the reality of death and its function as judgment. The Bible implies that judgment is a spur to conscience, which convicts us of sin and leads us to our need of repentance and redemption."[22]

Reincarnation

What if an individual fails to recognize his inherent divinity? For many New Agers, reincarnation is the answer to this psychic dilemma. Reincarnationists believe that the soul experiences multiple lives, gradually attaining a state of perfection in which oneness with the impersonal God of pantheism is realized.[23] Actress Shirley MacLaine recalls numerous past lives. MacLaine believes she once lived as "a young Buddhist monk, an orphan child adopted by a herd of elephants, a Colonial settler...during the signing of the U. S. Constitution, a ballet dancer in Russia, and a Mongolian maid raped by a bandit."[24]

Intrinsic to Eastern spirituality, regardless of the appearance of ethics or the sophisticated-sounding philosophy, is open idolatry, animism, and spiritism. New Age spirituality is nonhistorical and nonrevelational. Experience alone becomes the norm by which to test spiritual realities. The New Age mystic is left with an irrational form of spirituality based on a religious experience. For the New Age, the appeal of raw spiritual power squelches any concern to evaluate its legitimacy. Few bother to inquire after the source of spiritual expression.

5. ALL RELIGIONS ARE EQUAL ROADS TO GOD

Typical of New Age gurus is to paint all of the religions of the world with the same pantheistic brush. The claim of equality among religions and the belief that they ultimately, at their core, really teach the same thing is syncretism. Benjamin Creme, an "esotericist" and New Age spokesman, states:

Throughout history, humanity's evolution has been guided by a group of enlightened men, the Masters of Wisdom. They have remained largely in the remote desert and mountain places of earth, working mainly through disciples who live openly in the world. The message of the Christ's reappearance has been given primarily by such a disciple, trained for his task for over 20 years. At the center of this "spiritual Hierarchy" stands the World Teacher, Lord Maitreya, known by Christians as the Christ. And as Christians await the Second Coming, so the Jews await the Messiah, the Buddhists the fifth Buddha, the Moslems the Imam Mahdi, and the Hindus await Krishna. These are all names for one individual. His presence in the world guarantees there will be no third World War.[25]

Some parallels can be drawn among the religions of the world relative to their historical development and existing ethical standards; however, basic doctrinal tenets stand in great contrast among the religions of the world.

Contrary to former notions of the evolution of religion, some anthropologists and archeologists suggest that monotheism (the worship of one God) is the most ancient form of religious worship.[26] Among primitive religions, the one God has been replaced with many gods (polytheism) who eventually withdraw so far from man that they become inactive in the religious life of man. The gods are seen as disinheriting their earthly involvement to a son or a demiurge whose mission is to finish or perfect creation. Gradually religious practice degenerates further to the worship of mythical ancestors, mother-goddesses, the fecundating gods, and the like.[27] The evidence indicates a degeneracy from a true knowledge and worship of the one God.

The above-mentioned observations serve to demonstrate the religious schizophrenia that characterizes the syncretism of the New Age Movement. This can be shown by the following illustration:

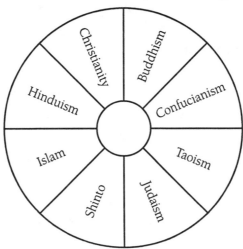

This circle graph represents the major religions of the world. Each of the major religions of the world claims to teach us something about ultimate reality and the relationship of man to that ultimate reality (God, cosmos, etc.). Inductively, we can eliminate many of the world's religions as legitimate because of their failure to conform to the evidence supporting monotheism. Buddhism is agnostic (philosophical view that insists we cannot know that there is a God). Confucianism is likewise agnostic. Hinduism is polytheistic. Taoism is characterized by metaphysical dualism. Metaphysical dualism is the religious concept of two eternal, impersonal forces; one is positive (Yang) and one is negative (Yin). The impersonal forces of Yang and Yin represent a degeneracy from, not a conformity to, monotheistic religion. Shintoism is henotheistic. Henotheism is the worship of one supreme or local deity. Henotheism acknowledges the existence of many gods in common with polytheism.

Islam is one of the three remaining monotheistic religions. However, Islam derives from both Judaism and Christianity. It follows then, that the newer "revelation" (the Koran) must conform to the older revelation (the Bible) in order to validate its truth claims. The God of the Bible (Yahweh) never changes because of his eternal nature (Malachi 3:6). It is irrational to conclude, therefore, that God would communicate something to one generation and then centuries later communicate something entirely different to another generation. Islam, however, makes such false claims.[28]

Finally, we come to Judaism and Christianity. Christianity is indebted to Judaism. Christianity inherited four fundamental concepts from Judaism:

(1) Monotheistic worship

(2) The personhood of God

(3) the concept of verbal revelation (the Bible)

(4) the idea that God intervenes in real, space-time human history.[29]

The Messiah is also from Jewish lineage. In the person of Jesus Christ, it can be demonstrated that Christianity is the fulfillment of the Mosaic Law and the Jewish prophets.[30]

The New Age disregards both history and basic doctrinal tenets in its efforts to syncretize the religions of the world. However, Christianity "is the only religion which purports to offer external, objective evidence of its validity. All other religions appeal to inner experience without any means of objective validation."[31]

The Christ of the New Age

David Spangler speaks of Christ in pagan-pantheistic terms:

> However, the Cosmic Christ did not come only for humanity, but in service to all evolving life streams of all the kingdoms of Nature upon the planet. Through the channel made for him by the human consciousness of Jesus, the Christ entered the very structure and life of Earth and united with his counterpart within the Earth Logos.[32]

Mark and Elizabeth Clare Prophet of the Church Universal and Triumphant are also representative of New Age thought's denial of the person of Jesus as Christ:

> The Master's greatest desire was that they should not mistake the son of Man [Jesus] for the Son of God [the

Christ]. Should confusion arise regarding the source of his humanity [in Christ] and the source of his divinity [in God], the Savior knew that generations to come would not worship the Christ, but the man Jesus.[33]

Benjamin Creme states that Jesus is divine "in exactly the sense that we are divine."[34] Speaking of Jesus, Creme further asserts that "He is Divine, having perfected Himself and manifested the Divinity potential in each of us."[35] Shirley MacLaine goes way out on a limb in her proclamation concerning the Son of God: "Christ was the most advanced human ever to walk on this planet."[36]

Many pantheists deny that Jesus died on the Cross: "Jesus did not sleep within the tomb."[37] Levi Dowling describes the resurrection of Jesus Christ in the occult tradition as a transmutation from "carnal flesh and blood to flesh of God."[38]

Occultists believe that Jesus went through degrees of initiation which are open to all men. Upon entering the world, Jesus was a third-degree "initiate." He became a fourth-degree "initiate" at his crucifixion and a fifth-degree "initiate" after his resurrection.

The Jesus of the Bible did not come into the world to show us that he was like God but rather to reveal to man that God was like him (John 1:18). Jesus Christ is the fullness of the Godhead in human flesh (Colossians 2:9). Therefore, Jesus is not merely an illuminated man, he is the incarnation of the living God (John 1:1, 14).

Connections/Networking/General Systems Theory

"Connections" is a New Age concept of the interconnectedness of all of the separate components in existence.[39] A university professor describes this concept as "a kind of magical circle, an unbroken unity with all life and cosmic processes, including my own life."[40]

Connections are intrinsic to New Age ideology. Connections are revered as the basis for the New Age perspective of holism. The ultimate expression of holism in the New Age is one unified sociopolitical world system. Marilyn Ferguson further explains:

> Because these connections can only be sustained by a flow of energy, the system is always in flux. Notice the paradox; the more coherent or intricately connected the structure, the most unstable it is. Increased coherence means increased instability! This very instability is the key to transformation. The dissipation of energy, as Prigogine demonstrated by his elegant mathematics, creates the potential for sudden reordering.[41]

A "sudden reordering" refers to the spiritual transformation of the earth resulting in the emergence of the New Age.

Connections provide a modem for "Networks." Jessica Lipnack and Jeffrey Stamps, coauthors of *Networking*, inform us that:

> Networks are composed of self-reliant and autonomous participants—people and organizations who simultaneously function as independent "wholes" and as interdependent "parts."[42]

Networking is like casting a net over the multitude of organizations and individuals within the New Age, interconnecting them for the purpose of information distribution.

Tielhard de Chardin, a patron saint among New Agers, believed in an expanding layer of consciousness that permeated the "noosphere." Chardin spoke of his noosphere as becoming a cultural reality: "Like the meridians as they approach the poles, science, philosophy and religion are bound to converge as they draw nearer to the whole."[43] Networks are seen as the reality of Chardin's dreams.

Networks shun bureaucratic or hierarchical configurations, emphasizing rather a decentralization of power in accomplishing global transformation.

> Just as a bureaucracy is less than the sum of its parts, a network is many times greater than the sum of its parts. This is a source of power never before tapped in history. Multiple self-sufficient social movements linked for a whole array of goals whose accomplishment would transform every aspect of contemporary life.[44]

Networks bring "like-minded" people together by "conferences, phone calls, air travel, books, phantom organizations, papers, pamphleteering, photocopying, lectures, workshops, parties, grapevines, mutual friends, summit meetings, coalitions, tapes, newsletters."[45] Because of an emphasis upon a decentralization of power there are "tens of thousands of entry points" into the web of networks that are intertwined throughout the multifaceted New Age movement.[46]

General Systems Theory is a related concept to networks. General Systems Theory presupposes the indivisible unity of the universe (monism). Every separate variable of any system is united with other variables like the links of a chain. Cause and effect are indistinguishable, according to this theory, because all variables are essentially one unified whole. This theory forms the basis for relationships, a sacred value in New Age thought.

The author of General Systems Theory, Ludwig von Bertalanffy, explains his view of all things in existence as one organic whole:

> It's applications range from the biophysics of cellular processes to the dynamics of populations, from the problems of physics to those of psychiatry and those of political and cultural units.
>
> General Systems Theory is symptomatic of a change in our worldview. No longer do we see the world in a blind play of atoms, but rather a great organization.[47]

Syntropy (the Greek prefix *syn* means "together with") is a term applied in New Age ideology to the increasing organization of relationships within the systems of the universe. This concept is critical to the New Age value of the interconnectedness of all components within the universe.

A Paradigm Shift

In order for a new planetary culture to emerge, New Agers insist that we must first experience a paradigm shift. A paradigm is a conceptual model used for the interpretation of human experience. The transformation that the New Age seeks is the orientation of humanity to its own worldview (paradigm) and brand of spirituality.

Physicist Fritjof Capra is among many intellectuals who see modern man as the vanguard of the new world order. Capra points to numerous global crises in order to stress the need for a transformation of consciousness among humanity:

More than fifteen million people—most of them children—die of starvation each year; another 500 million are seriously undernourished. Almost 40 percent of the world's population has no access to professional health services; yet developing countries spend more than three times as much on armaments as on health care. Thirty-five percent of humanity lacks safe drinking water, while half of its scientists and engineers are engaged in the technology of making weapons.[48]

Modern man is incapable of dealing with complex social ills such as inflation, psychoses, disease, famine, and crime. Capra uses this as evidence to indict former ways of thinking, stressing that they are obsolete. Modern man needs new modes of thought in order to capably address and resolve the problems of today's world. Marilyn Ferguson agrees with Capra:

We try to solve problems with our existing tools, in their old context, instead of seeing that the escalating crisis is a symptom of our essential wrongheadedness.[49]

As the minds of humanity are transformed and, "When the moon is in the seventh house, and Jupiter aligns with Mars; then peace will guide the planets, and love will steer the stars."[50] This, according to New Agers, will climax in the birth of the New Age, a planetary paradise.

The conception and birth of this new worldview can be more fully understood by examining the historical process of Western man's exaltation and final rejection of reason. The escape from reason has resulted in modern man's unrestrained acceptance of occult mysticism.

A COMPARISON OF WORLDVIEWS

NEW AGE WORLDVIEW

Reality—The universe is one essential, undifferentiated whole (Monism). Unlike Hinduism the material world does exist. However, it is a transmaterial universe.

God—God is impersonal and is contained within all of existence (pantheism). Material reality is imbued with consciousness. God is all that really exists.

Man—Man, as a part of the one reality, is inherently divine. God is individualized in man. Man has evolved to a position of supremacy over the rest of existence.

Ethics—Man is good by nature. Through cosmic consciousness, categories of moral good and evil are transcended.

BIBLICAL WORLDVIEW

God created the universe and all things within it (including man) from nothing (ex nihilo; Genesis 1; Isaiah 45:18–19). All things were created through the Word (John 1:1–3). An intelligent creation gives meaning and purpose to the universe.

God is personal. He is both transcendent over his creation (Psalm 103:19) and immanent in relationship to creation (Psalm 72:19). The glory of God is revealed through his creation (Romans 1:19, 20), and yet to confuse God with his creation is scripturally condemned (Romans 1:25).

The God of the Bible is the only true God (Isaiah 43:10; Jeremiah 10:10, 11). Man is highly exalted because of special creation in God's image (Genesis 1:26). The New Age looks within and worships the image, which is idolatry (Exodus 20:5; Romans 1:23).

Morality is centered in man. The Bible views good and evil in antitheses. Revelation condemns the synthesizing of good and evil (Isaiah 5:20, 21). God is the absolute, transcendent moral standard as revealed in his Word. Man is in a condition of sin (Romans 3:23) and in need of a Savior (John 3:16; Hebrews 7:25).

NEW AGE WORLDVIEW

BIBLICAL WORLDVIEW

Revelation—Propositional revelation is a barrier to spiritual enlightenment. Direct mystical states are the norm in the New Age.

Propositional revelation (Bible) is verbally inspired (2 Timothy 3:16). Biblical revelation is historical. Therefore, Christianity can be tested relative to truth claims. Christianity is a relational faith which is intellectually defensible. Revelation leads to true spirituality.

History—History is cyclical. Man creates and directs the course of history independent of any transcendent reality.

The infinite God interecedes in space, time, and history. God orders history in fulfillment of his purposes. Man is significant in history and is a part of God's destined plan. History is meaningful.

Salvation—Man needs a transformation of consciousness (cosmic consciousness). Apart from cosmic consciousness, reincarnation is necessary. Man must save himself. Death is an illusion.

The heart of man is desperately wicked through sin (Jeremiah 17:9). Jesus Christ is God incarnate (John 1:1, 14). Man must be transformed (born again) through Jesus Christ (John 3:3). Man is saved by grace (Ephesians 2:8). Death followed by judgment is a reality (Hebrews 9:27).

World Religions—All roads lead to God. There is no basis for comparative religions. All religions emanate from the same source.

Religious syncretism is irrational, for all religions do not teach the same things. This denies a common source for the world's religions.

Eschatology—Man will give birth to the New Age through his own consciousness (occult view of reality). Man is aided by spirit "guides" in his quest to consciously create a new heaven and a new earth.

The Second Coming of the Lord Jesus Christ will result in the new heaven and the new earth under this righteous reign (Revelation 21:1–8). Spirit "guides" are malignant spiritual entities (demons) that deliver spiritual delusion and a rejection of the one true God (2 Thessalonians 2:8–12).

WINNING OVER
SATAN'S SHENANIGANS

CHARLES C. RYRIE

Charles C. Ryrie, Th.D., Ph.D
General Editor—Ryrie Study Bible
Professor of Systematic Theology Emeritus
Dallas Theological Seminary
Author

According to the dictionary, a wile is "a trick or stratagem, a sly artifice, deceit." The wiles of Satan are a major concern for the Christian who would live a spiritual life. And yet, as in other areas of the spiritual life, this too is a matter which needs balance. There are some believers who see Satan at work in every detail of life; others fail to recognize his activity at all. Some, strange to say, actually or at least practically deny his real existence. Apparently there are those who feel that Satan merely exists in the mind of man; therefore, the fact that we think he exists is the only genuine existence he has. However, the Scriptures teach that Satan was alive before man was ever created; thus he existed before there was a human mind to conceive of or recognize his existence (Ezekiel 28:13–15). Furthermore, every reference by our Lord to the evil one is a proof of his real existence (Matthew 13:39; 25:41;

Luke 10:18; John 12:31; 16:11), or else one is forced to conclude that Christ did not know what He was talking about. Of course, modern theology explains these references as Christ accommodating Himself to the ignorance of the people of His day; but such accommodation, if it were so, would invalidate His entire message. Satan exists. The Bible and our Lord attest to that fact.

But—getting back to the wiles or tricks of Satan—how can Satan be so clever? There are at least three factors that contribute to his mastery of the art of trickery. For one thing, he belongs to an order of creatures that is higher than man (Hebrews 2:7). He is an angel, though fallen now, and among the angels he was a cherub (Ezekiel 28:14). This would seem to give Satan a constitutional superiority over man.

For another thing, Satan's experience is far greater than any man's could ever be. By this very longevity Satan has acquired a breadth and depth of experience which he matches against the limited knowledge of man. He has observed other believers in every conceivable situation, thus enabling him to predict with accuracy how we will respond to circumstances. Although Satan is not omniscient, his wide experience and observation of man throughout his entire history on earth give him knowledge which is far superior to anything any man could have. Apparently, too, Satan knows the Bible; therefore, a believer has no particular advantage over him in this area either.

A third advantage Satan has is his ability to transform himself in a variety of ways. These vary all the way from presenting himself as an angel of light and his ministers as ministers of righteousness (2 Corinthians 11:14–15) to showing himself as a dragon with horns and a tail (Revelation 12:3). Although this latter representation is often said not to be in the Bible, it is; and it is there to help us realize the fierceness of Satan's nature as he engages in a death struggle with God's people.

To sum it up: Satan because of his constitutional superiority, his great knowledge, and his chameleon character is a foe whose wiles are not to be taken lightly by any Christian.

SATAN'S PLAN

From the time of his first sin until his final defeat, Satan's plan and purpose have been, are, and always will be to seek to establish a rival rule to God's kingdom. He is promoting a system of which he is the head and which stands in opposition to God and His rule in the universe.

But to carry forward this program, Satan uses a plan which is extremely deceptive because of its subtlety. Instead of promoting a kingdom whose characteristics are exactly opposite to the features of God's rule, he seeks to counterfeit God's program in the world. Counterfeiting the will of God has been, presently is, and always will be his plan as long as he has freedom.

Of course, counterfeiting has a single purpose, and that is to create something as similar to the original as possible and to do it by means of a shortcut. If you were going to counterfeit dollar bills, you would be foolish to put Lincoln's picture on them, for that would obviously show them up as counterfeit. You would place Washington's picture on them so as to make them as similar to the genuine article as possible. But you would take some shortcut—perhaps a less accurate and thus imperfect engraving—thus revealing your work as counterfeit to the experts. But in all features of their appearance, the bills would have to appear to be just the same as genuine ones.

Satan's plan is a counterfeit plan to God's, and this is the most important fact to know about all of his purposes in this world. If you grasp this, then you will be well on the way to a successful defense against him. If not, it will be all the more easy for him to deceive you. He is a master counterfeiter, and he is trying to promote something that is similar, not dissimilar, to the plan and will of God. Satan, with all of his intelligence and long experience, knows that if he puts something which is clearly evil in the path of a Christian, he is apt to be alert to the fact that this comes from Satan and as a consequence be on guard against it. But if Satan can offer something which though good in itself is not the best, he will be more likely to gain the victory over the believer.

Satan boldly announced this counterfeit policy when he first sinned. In Isaiah 14:14 (KJV) it is recorded of him that he declared his opposition to God this way: "I will be like the most High." There is a counterfeit—like, not unlike, the Most High.

We have already examined how Satan pawned this off on Adam and Eve in the Garden of Eden in Genesis 3. He offered Eve the tantalizing prize of being like God, knowing good and evil, by enticing her to take something which was good for food, pleasant to the eyes, and productive of knowledge. It all seemed good, except that eating of that fruit was contrary to the revealed will of God.

At the temptation of Christ, Satan tried the same counterfeiting approach. The offer of food was not inherently evil. The suggestion that Christ cast Himself off the pinnacle of the temple without doing Himself harm would have brought Him (had He done it) recognition from the people which was entirely right that He have. To have the kingdoms of the world is His prerogative, and He will rule over them in a future day. Actually the items Satan offered Christ (sustenance, recognition and power) were not wrong in themselves nor were they things Christ should not have had. What was wrong was the way Satan was tempting our Lord with these things; for he was trying to obtain these glories without the suffering involved, particularly the suffering of His death on the cross. The ends Satan offered were right and proper for Christ to have; but the means involved a shortcut, bypassing the cross. It was a clever counterfeit, and completely in line with Satan's usual method.

As we come to the end of this age, Satan through his demons is promoting false doctrine (1 Timothy 4:1) with the purpose of producing false doctrine (2 Timothy 3:5). Here is another counterfeit—a semblance of godliness, but that which leaves out the power of God.

But doesn't Satan promote evil, too? Yes, he does. Ananias and Sapphira's lying hypocrisy was induced by Satan (Acts 5:3), and infidelity is a temptation from Satan (1 Corinthians 7:5). And, of course, all of his "good" counterfeits are evil. The point to remember is that Satan will do anything and everything he can to detract from the will of God. Counterfeiting in the form of substituting something seemingly good for the plan of God is likely his preferred way of doing things, but he cannot always exercise his preference. So he will do anything he can and work against people in any way, at any point and on any level he can whether that means using evil or "good."

SATAN'S DEVICES

In carrying out his design to counterfeit the plan of God, Satan has many devices which he uses. Furthermore, he will employ them at any time and in any variety and combination of ways. But to be forewarned is to be forearmed.

1. We have already emphasized that Satan is the master counterfeiter. This is the device of deceit. Another example of this tactic is his sowing of tares among the wheat in this age (Matthew 13:24–30, 36–42). Tares are the plant known as the "bearded darnel" which in the blade is indistinguishable from wheat. Since tares are unsuitable as human food they must be separated from the wheat, which can be done with greater ease when the grain matures. Sowing tares in a field for purposes of revenge was a crime under the Roman government. In the parable, our Lord likens the tares which Satan sows to children of the devil, while the wheat symbolizes the children of God. In sowing the two together in the field (which is the world), the devil today deceives many. People who are in reality tares may be deceived into thinking they are wheat because they have made a profession of Christianity and exhibit some of the characteristics of believers. This gives them a false sense of security. Undoubtedly there are many tares sitting in church pews and serving on church boards who do not realize that they are headed for "a furnace of fire" where "there shall be wailing and gnashing of teeth" (Matthew 13:42, KJV). I often think that Satan is far more satisfied with unsaved people who are in church on Sunday morning than with those who may be playing golf or sleeping off a hangover, for they are more apt to think that they are all right, whereas those not in church might have some sense or feeling that all is not well. This is one of the ways Satan deceives the world.

2. Sometimes Satan employs open opposition to the work of God in order to thwart its progress. There are several examples of this in the Bible.

When Paul was in Corinth writing his first letter back to the Thessalonians he expressed his desire to return to Thessalonica to strengthen the young church; but, said he, "Satan hindered us" (1 Thessalonians 2:18, KJV). This hindrance apparently refers to the security, or bail, which Jason had to guarantee and which involved an agreement that Paul would not return to that city again and become a public nuisance (Acts 17:9). Paul saw this action on the part of the rulers of Thessalonica as an action of Satan.

Sometime later, the risen Lord warned the church at Smyrna: "The devil shall cast some of you into prison, that ye may be tried" (Revelation 2:10, KJV). Here was open opposition instigated by Satan using unbelievers to seize some of the believers and imprison them.

At the same time the church at Pergamum was said to dwell "where Satan's seat [throne]" was (Revelation 2:13). This could refer either to the worship of the Roman emperor, or to the worship of Zeus at his magnificent altar on the Acropolis, or to the worship of the Greek gods in the temple. Or, of course, Satan's throne could be a reference to all three forms of pagan worship. The point is that in this instance Satan's open opposition to the gospel was in the form of false religion—a tactic which he is still using today in the form of both antichristian religious and so-called "Christian" cults. The form of the ritual may be very beautiful, the standards may even be moral, but if the saving death of Jesus Christ is left out, it is a false, satanic system.

3. In promoting his ends, whether deceptively or openly, Satan often employs a systematic theology to appeal to the intellectual pride of man. The church at Thyatira was warned about accepting the deep teachings of Satan (Revelation 2:24). Apparently a false prophetess in that church (whose actual name may or may not have been Jezebel) was promoting immorality and idolatry (v. 20) by incorporating these sins within a doctrinal system

which probably made them appear as not sinful. Paul warned that
the last days will be characterized by "doctrines of devils" (1 Timothy 4:1, KJV), which, oddly enough, will include teaching asceticism
as a means of trying to please God and gain His favor. Abstention,
rather than indulgence, will be part of the satanic systematic theology of the last days.

It has sometimes been said that more likely one will find Satan
at work in a seminary than in a bar. Undoubtedly he will work
wherever he sees opportunities, but perhaps he needs to be less
concerned about the bar, where man's own lusts will automatically
take over, than about the seminary, where he fights for the minds of
men and, if successful, can poison the stream at its source.

4. One of the most frequently used devices of Satan is the
applying of pressure on the believer in various ways. It may be
pressure that arises from the inability to maintain a good course
of action. This was true of some women who have embarked on
a life of self-denial which proved to be too severe for them. In
their failure they had followed Satan. The pressure of that life of
self-denial was too great, and the embarrassment that would have
resulted from admitting it too overwhelming; so they yielded to
satanic pressure (1 Timothy 5:14–15).

In another instance, Paul warned that Satan could easily turn
the proper remorse of a sin-burdened conscience into an occasion
of further sin (2 Corinthians 2:11). To prevent this the church
needed not only to forgive but also to restore the brother who had
confessed and turned from his sin. Otherwise Satan might be able
to put the man under the pressure of continued self-accusation
which would lead him into more sin. Continued introspection
can often be the opening wedge for additional satanic pressure on
the believer.

These two examples show that pressures can come from personally stepping out of the will of God (1 Timothy 5) or from others not doing His will (2 Corinthians 2). Often Satan does not have to enter the picture early or even frequently, since we can be led astray of our own lusts or be involved in a circumstance not of our own making. Pride or covetousness will sometimes lead the believer to seek to acquire something which of itself is neither good nor bad. But to gain it may require extra work which may lead to the neglect of the family which in turn will bring pressures that Satan can use to defeat that Christian. Too, the circumstances of twentieth-century life are so increasingly complex as to demand more and more guidance from the Lord so that an individual knows when to say yes and when to say no, so that he avoids exposing himself to pressure which Satan might use as a leverage against him. We may be sure of one thing—he will use every advantage we give him.

5. Others of his devices (some of which we shall look at later in more detail) include discouragement, sidetract, temptation, stagnation and, of course, any ruse which would keep the believer from normal and proper maturity in the spiritual life.

THE BELIEVER'S DEFENSE

All too frequently people run to one of two extremes in their thinking about Satan and his attacks on the believer. Some become overoccupied with him and as a result see Satan actively and intimately concerned with every problem or situation that goes wrong in their lives. I heard recently of a young Christian athlete who, every time he missed a shot, felt that he was out of the will of God and under attack by Satan. With help like this Satan received credit for many feats he really has nothing to do with. We need to remember that within our own beings is the capacity to initiate, promote and commit sin. Mix in the world with the sin nature and there are two enemies which are more than able to overpower the Christian without involving Satan. Overoccupation with Satan can also lead to morbid introspection in which not only every action but also every motive is minutely examined in the light of Satan's possible connection. On the other hand, this undue concern with Satan can sometimes provide a person with unjustified excuses for his actions. "Oh, Satan did it" becomes an out for the person to relieve himself of responsibility for the action, and not against his will.

In contrast to overoccupation with Satan, there is the opposite attitude which underestimates his activity in the believer's life. Undoubtedly Satan is pleased when he can promote such deception, for if the believer does not recognize the source of the problem as being Satan, he cannot attack it in the right way. The trend today to seek to explain everything in terms of natural phenomena has without doubt provided Satan with a mask under which to work. For instance, personal emotional difficulties, church problems, adverse circumstances are seldom attributed to Satan. Indeed, to do so almost seems foolish, but it may be more foolish not to do so!

Somewhere between these two extremes lies a proper balance, but achieving it is not always easy. We need to be alert to all of Satan's possible devices, for he is at work attacking, deceiving, counterfeiting and seeking to defeat the believer at every opportunity. Thank God we are not left defenseless. Provision has been made to meet his attacks.

1. In two places in the New Testament we are told that the Lord Jesus lives in heaven to make intercession for His children

(Romans 8:34; Hebrews 7:25). Apparently this work of praying for us has two aspects: curative and preventive. The curative is necessary to sustain fellowship when we sin (1 John 2:1); the preventive helps keep us from sinning, particularly when attacked by Satan. The Lord gave us an insight into this in a petition He made just before His crucifixion when He said to the Father, "I pray not that thou shouldest take them out of the world, but that thou shouldest keep them from the evil" (John 17:15, KJV). The word *evil* as it appears in this verse can be either neuter (evil things) or masculine (evil one—Satan). The latter is the meaning John seems to prefer in his writings (cf, 1 John 2:13–14; 3:12; 5:18–19). Thus Christ is asking the Father to keep believers from Satan. What this means in terms of sparing us from attacks of Satan we cannot know fully this side of heaven, but there we may learn all that the intercessory work of our Lord has meant on our behalf in defeating our adversary. This, of course, is a defense which He does entirely for us; we have no part except to receive its benefits.

2. A second line of defense for the believer is to know that the purposes of God may on occasion include using Satan to teach a particular lesson. In such instances our defense is to learn the lesson God has for us even though He may be using Satan in the process of teaching it. That was, of course, what God did in the case of Job when He permitted Satan to be used to carry out His own purposes in Job's life. A similar thing happened in Paul's life (2 Corinthians 12:7–10) when the Lord sent a messenger of Satan to inflict some kind of "thorn in the flesh" on him in order to keep him from getting proud over the revelations God had given him. The lesson Paul learned was the sufficiency of God's grace. Reliance on that was the only way he could defeat Satan and submit to the will of God. Such involvement of the will of God, Satan and the

believer at the same time is often inscrutable; yet it happens.

3. It is always a primary importance in defeating Satan to take the proper attitude in relation to him. Though we have the power of God on our side, it is never wise to assume that victory is automatically guaranteed. To remember that we are engaging a mighty foe, the greatest of all of God's creatures, is to assume a proper attitude toward Satan. The example of this is recorded in Jude 9 where we are reminded that even as great an angel as Michael the archangel did not dare take on Satan alone but called on the Lord to rebuke him. No Christian, then, should ever feel that he is wise enough or powerful enough to engage Satan apart from complete dependence on the Lord.

4. A definite stand against Satan on the part of the believer is essential for victory. Why say this? Is it not self-evident? Yes, it is, but many Christians will never realize victory over the devil simply because they have never decided to take a stand against him. They are still flirting with the sin or temptation Satan puts in their path. They may even pray earnestly for victory and piously speak of their desire for relief, but in their hearts is still the desire to indulge and yield if only occasionally to some pet sin. Only a definite decision stand against the wicked one can ever put them on the road to victory.

James wrote of this, using a verb tense that means to take a decisive stand, when he said, "Resist the devil, and he will flee from you" (4:7, KJV). Likewise, the believer's armor is given in order that he might take a stand against his adversary (Ephesians 6:11, 13–14). Such a stand is vital as a base of operations on which to wage the continual warfare that comes; without it there can be only retreat and defeat. With it there can be victory, though not without continued warfare.

5. A rather simple and concise formula for defeating Satan is given in Revelation 12:11 (KJV): "And they overcame him by the blood of the Lamb, and by the word of their testimony; and they loved not their lives unto the death." There are three elements in the formula. The first, the basis of all victory over Satan, is the blood of the Lamb. This is not some mystical or even magical application of nearly literal blood today as the believer "claims" it or "dips" into its reservoir. The blood of the Lamb was shed on a hill outside Jerusalem, and that became the clear evidence of death having occurred. The blood is not in heaven; the crucified Christ is, and as such He has defeated Satan (Colossians 2:15). And His victory makes our victory possible. This is what is meant by overcoming Satan by the blood of the Lamb.

The second element in the formula is something we can do to make Christ's victory applicable in our lives—be positive and consistent in our testimony for the Lord. It is a fatal mistake to believe that while faith in the death of Christ is required, testimony for Christ is optional. No testimony by both life and mouth means no defeat for Satan. The Lord reminded His disciples: "Ye are the light of the world. A city that is set on a hill cannot be hid. Neither do men light a candle, and put it under a bushel, but on a candlestick; and it giveth light unto all that are in the house" (Matthew 5:14–15, KJV). Like the candle under a bushel, a testimony hidden under cowardice, compromise, worldliness or indifferent neglect will be extinguished. Sometimes (and I hope I am not misunderstood in saying this) a defeated Christian does not need to pray more or read his Bible more—he needs to be out witnessing more.

The third feature of this formula for victory is a basic attitude toward life itself—an attitude or self-sacrifice to the point of being perfectly willing to die for Christ. An attitude like this will put one's set of values in life in right perspective more quickly than anything else. Defeating Satan requires a martyr spirit. "Whosoever will save his life shall lose it; but whosoever shall lose his life for my sake and the gospel's, the same shall save it" (Mark 8:35, KJV).

6. Finally, victory over Satan requires the constant use of the armor which God has provided for the Christian (Ephesians 6:11–18). This includes truth which, like a girdle, holds everything together and gives proper orientation to life. This, of course, is the truth of God, not the wisdom of men, and it needs to be the basis for how we look at everything. Finances and friendships, activities and attitudes, family and fun, science and psychology must all be governed by the truth of God as revealed in the Scriptures.

Righteousness is the breastplate to guard the vital organs of life. Is this the imputed righteousness we have by being in Christ? Of course. Is this the imparted righteousness which we live in daily life? Of course. Both are meant, for a righteous life has to be based on a righteous position, and a righteous position that does not manifest itself in godly living is probably not genuine.

Our feet should be prepared to do the will and work of God because we have experienced the pace of God which the gospel brings. No stumbling and no slowing down should characterize the believer.

Faith is the large shield that gives overall protection. This is not simply faith in the crises of life, but faith to overcome the tempter in the routine of life. We walk by faith and not by sight.

Around the head goes the helmet of salvation. How many Christians seem to feel that they need saving only from the neck down! We have already noticed that the dedicated life begins with the renewing of the mind (Romans 12:2); our thought life needs to experience the effects of salvation.

The single offensive weapon is the sword of the Spirit which is the word of God. This is not simply the written Word, for the particular word used here and translated "word" means spoken word. The sword of the Spirit then, is the spoken proclamation of the written Word. It is not simply a New Testament carried in one's pocket, however good that may be; rather, it is the spoken testimony which we give with our lips. The sword of the Spirit of Ephesians 6:17 is the word of testimony of Revelation 12:11.

The final feature of the armor is prayer, not just mouthing of petitions, but Spirit-guided prayer.

This is the armor provided for our protection, but God will not forcibly dress us in it. We have the responsibility to take it up (v. 13), and it will be a lifetime involvement. To be sure, we can put it all on in a moment, but developing skillful use of it requires a lifetime of practice. We may be sure too that Satan will seek to find the chinks in our armor in his unceasing and relentless fight against us.

Let me conclude this chapter on the wiles of the devil by reminding you of parts of three verses which a speaker paraphrased and put together for me many years ago, and which have been a source of real assurance: "Christ lives in me" (Galatians 2:20); "Greater is he that is in [me] than he who is in the world" (1 John 4:4); "He will never leave me, nor forsake me" (Hebrews 13:5). Our Lord is our victory. Trust Him and use all the means He has provided to defeat the great enemy of our souls.

THE AWESOME POWER
OF PRAYER

RAY C. STEDMAN

Ray C. Stedman
Pastor, speaker and author
(deceased)

The apostle Paul has outlined for us steps we must take if we expect to be strong in the Lord and to resist the attacks of Satan. The first is to put on the armor of God—the *whole* armor—"that you may be able to stand against the wiles of the devil."

And the second step, Paul says, is to pray.

> Pray at all times in the Spirit, with all prayer and supplication. To that end keep alert with all perseverance, making supplication for all the saints, and also for me, that utterance may be given me in opening my mouth boldly to proclaim the mystery of the gospel, for which I am an ambassador in chains; that I may declare it boldly, as I ought to speak. (Ephesians 6:18–20, RSV)

There is a very strong and powerful relationship between putting on the armor of God and praying. These two things belong together; in fact, one grows out of the other. It is not enough to put on the armor of God—you must also pray. It is not enough to pray—you must also have put on the armor of God.

Putting on the armor of God is far from being merely figurative—it is an actual thing you do. It is remembering what Christ is to you and thinking through the implications of that relationship in terms of your present struggle and experience. Essentially, putting on the armor is done in the realm of your thought-life. It is an adjustment of the attitude of your heart to reality, to things as they really are. It is thinking through the implications of the facts revealed in God's Word.

Our problem with life is that we do not see it as it is; we suffer from strange illusions. This is why we desperately need and must have the revelation of the facts of Scripture. Life is what God has declared it to be. When we face it on that basis, we discover that revelation is right, it is accurate, it does describe what is happening. And more, it tells why things happen and what lies behind them. All this is part of putting on this armor, of appropriating Christ to life in terms of your present situation. It is all done in the realm of the thought-life.

What do you do when you put on the breastplate of righteousness? You think of Christ and what his righteousness means as it is imparted to you. What do you do when you take up the sword of the spirit? You give heed to those flashes of Scripture, those portions of the Word of God that come to your mind and have immediate application to the situation you are facing. But again, this is all done in the realm of thought.

At first it takes time to work this all through, but as we learn how to do it, the process becomes much more rapid. We can almost instantaneously think through this line of approach to the problems we are facing. This is what Paul means in the letter to the Corinthians when he says, "take every thought captive to obey Christ" (2 Corinthians 10:5, RSV).

HARMFUL IF NOT APPLIED

If we merely think about these things, however, and never bring our thoughts into fulfillment through some form of action, we are actually violating our basic humanity, and this can be dangerous. Human beings are made both to *think* and to *do*—in that order. We receive information first, assimilate it, correlate it, and think it through. And then we act upon what we have both thought and felt. Our emotions and our mind, working upon our will, bring us at last to activity. This is the normal and proper procedure for human living.

All our doing must and will grow out of our thinking. Sometimes we speak of "thoughtless" actions. We say of someone that he acted thoughtlessly. This is impossible. You cannot act thoughtlessly. What we really mean is that someone has acted with very superficial, shallow thinking. But it is actually impossible ever to act without having first thought. Yet it is possible to think without ever acting. That is what the apostle is bringing us to in 2 Corinthians 10:5.

To think without doing is inevitably frustrating. It is like cooking and never eating. You can imagine how frustrating that would be. So the complement to putting on the armor of God and the activity which results from it is to pray. First to think through and then to pray.

Notice that the apostle does not reverse this and instruct us to pray first and then put on the armor of God. That is what we often try to do, and the result is a feeble, impotent prayer life. There is great practical help here if we follow carefully the designated order of Scripture.

I think most Christians, if they were honest, would confess that they were dissatisfied with their prayer life. They feel it is inadequate and perhaps infrequent. All of us at times struggle to improve the quality as well as the quantity of our prayer lives. Sometimes we adopt schedules that we attempt to maintain or we develop long lists of names and projects and places that we try to remember in prayer or we attempt to discipline ourselves in some way to a greater ministry in this realm. In other words, we begin with the doing, but when we do that, we are starting in the wrong place. We are violating our basic human nature in doing it that way. The place to start is not with the doing but with the thinking.

THE PLACE TO START

Now I am not suggesting that there is no place for Christian discipline. There is. I am not suggesting that we won't need to take our wills and put them to a task and follow through. There is this need. But first we should do what is involved in "putting on the armor of God." First think through the implications of our faith, and then prayer will follow naturally and much more easily. It will be thoughtful prayer—that has meaning and relevance.

That is the problem with much of our praying now, is it not? It is so shallow and superficial. What is needed? Prayer should be an outgrowth of thoughtfulness about the implications of faith. That adds depth and significance to it. Prayer should be pointed and purposeful.

Now, basically what is prayer? Is it a mere superstition as some people think, a mumbling, a talking to yourself under the deluded dream that you are addressing deity? Or is it a form of black magic by which some heavenly genie is expected to manipulate life to our desire—a kind of ecclesiastical Aladdin's lamp that we rub? I am afraid many have that concept of prayer. On the other hand, is it, as certain groups tell us, self-communion, a psychological form of talking to yourself in which you discover depths in your being that were there all the time, but you did not realize it until you prayed?

All of these ideas of prayer hold no similarity with what we read in Scripture on the subject. Paul here recognizes two categories of prayer: that which he calls (1) all prayer, and (2) supplication. All prayer is the widest classification; supplication is the specific request that is made in prayer. And if you take the whole range of Bible teaching on this great subject of prayer, you will find that underlying all the biblical presentation of prayer is the idea that it is conversation with God. That is all it is; prayer is simply conversing with God.

FAMILY TALK

As we understand the position of a Christian, a believer, he is in the family of God. Therefore prayer is family talk. It is a friendly, intimate, frank, unrestricted talking with God, and it is into this close and intimate relationship that every individual is brought by faith in Jesus Christ. By faith in Christ we pass out of the realm of being strangers to God and aliens to the family of God into the intimate family circle of the children of God. It is easy to talk within a family circle, but think what harm is done to that intimacy if people refuse to talk within the family circle.

Now supplication is making some specific request. James says, "You do not have, because you do not ask" (James 4:2). In our conversation with God it is perfectly proper to ask, because we are children and he is a Father. What Paul is saying is, "After you have put on the armor of God, after you have thought through the implications of your faith in the ways that have been suggested previously, then talk to God about it." Tell him the whole thing. Tell him your reactions, tell him how you feel, describe your relationship to those around you and your reactions to them, and ask him for what you need.

Prayer is often considered to be such a high and holy thing that it has to be carried on in some artificial language or tone of voice. You hear this frequently from pulpits. Pastors adopt what has been aptly called a "stained-glass voice." They pray as though God were far off in some distant corner of the universe. But prayer is a simple conversation with a Father. It is what the apostle describes beautifully in the Epistle to the Philippians:

> Have no anxiety about anything, but in everything by prayer and supplication [there it is again] with thanksgiving let your requests be made known to God. And the peace of God, which passes all understanding, will keep your hearts and your minds in Christ Jesus. (Philippians 4:6–7).

That is a wonderful study in prayer. Paul is saying there are three simple things involved in prayer. First, worry about nothing: "Be anxious for nothing." Christian friends, do you hear what that says? Worry about nothing! This is one of the major problems in Christian living today.

Christians are either stumbling blocks to non-Christians or are a glowing testimony and witness to them depending on whether they worry or not. Christians are continually exhorted in Scripture to worry about nothing. Now that doesn't mean not to have a proper interest and concern about things. Stoicism is not advocated here, but we are not to be anxious, fretful, worried.

Nevertheless this is so often the attitude of our lives. Someone said, "I am so loaded up with worries that if anything happened to me this week it would be two weeks before I could get around to worrying about it." Sometimes we make an artificial attempt to cure our worrying by will power. As another has put it,

I've joined the new "Don't worry" Club
And now I hold my breath
I'm so scared I'm going to worry
That I'm worried half to death.

But the admonition is, Worry about nothing, and that is only possible when you have put on the armor of God. Do not try to attempt it on any other basis. Worry comes from fear, and the only thing that will dissolve fear is facts. Therefore to put on the armor of God is to face the facts. Therefore to put on the armor of God is to face the facts just as they are.

The second thing Paul says is involved in prayer is to pray about everything. *Everything!* Someone says, do you mean that God is interested in little things as well as big things? Is there anything that is big to God? They are all little things to him. Of course he is interested in them; he says so. The hairs on our head are numbered by him. Jesus was at great pains to show us that God is infinitely involved in the most minute details of our lives. He is concerned about everything. Therefore pray about everything.

And what is the result? "You will be kept through anything!"

That is what he says in Philippians. "The peace of God, which passes all understanding." It is a peace which no one can explain, which is there despite the circumstances, and which certainly does not arise out of any change of circumstances. And it "will keep your hearts and your minds in Christ Jesus." Can there be anything more relevant than that in this troubled, anxious, fretful, weary, disturbed world?

AN ESSENTIAL LINK

Inherent in prayer are three basic facts. When we pray we recognize first the existence of an invisible kingdom. We would never pray at all if we did not have some awareness that someone is listening, that behind what is visible there is an invisible kingdom. It is not far off in space somewhere; it is right here. It surrounds us on every side. We are constantly in touch with it even though we do not always realize it. It lies behind the facade of life, and all through the Scripture we are exhorted to take heed of this, to reckon with it and deal with it, to acknowledge that it exists.

The second thing that prayer reveals is that we Christians have confidence that the kingdom of God is highly significant, that it affects our lives directly, that the visible things which occur in our world are a direct result of something that is happening in the realm of invisibility. Therefore if you want to change the visibilities, you must start with the invisibilities.

Third, and perhaps the most hotly contested fact by the devil and his forces, is that our prayers play a direct and essential part in bringing God's invisible power to bear on visible life. In other words, God answers prayer. Prayer is purposeful and powerful. It is not pitiful and pathetic pleading with only a rare chance that it might be answered. No, prayer is powerful. God answers! Prayer is an essential link in the working of God in the world today. Without it he often does not work—with it he certainly does. Those three things are all involved in the matter of prayer.

But now we must immediately add that God answers prayer according to his promises. There is a very vague and undefined concept of prayer held by many that God answers any kind of prayer, no matter what you want or how you ask for it. This, of course, results frequently in disappointments and gives rise to the widespread belief that prayer is ineffectual. But God answers every prayer that is based upon a promise.

Prayer does not start with us; it starts with God. God must say he will do something before we are free to ask him to do it. That is the point. That is how it works with a father and his children. No parent commits himself to give his children anything they want or anything they ask for. He makes it clear to them that he will do certain things and not do other things. In the realm of those limits the father commits himself to answer his children's requests. So it is with God. God has given promises, and then they form the only proper basis for supplication.

This is what is meant here by Paul's reminder that we are to pray at all times in the Spirit. In the Spirit! Here again is a great area of misunderstanding. Many take the phrase "in the Spirit" to be descriptive of the emotions we should have when we pray. They think it is necessary to be greatly moved before prayer can be effectual—that we must always pray with deep earnestness. This is of course possible at times, but it is not essential or necessary to the effectiveness of prayer. And it is certainly not the meaning of this phrase "in the Spirit." It has no relationship to the emotions that we feel in prayer.

IF HE PROMISED

Well, what is it then? It means to pray according to the promises which the Spirit has given, and it is based on the character of God which the Spirit has made known. That is praying in the Spirit. God has never promised to answer just any prayer, but he does promise to answer prayer in a way that he has carefully outlined and given to us. He does so invariably and without partiality; he is no respecter of persons in this matter of prayer. In the realm of our personal needs (those needs that call forth most of our prayers)—the need of wisdom, perhaps, or power or patience or grace or strength—God's promise is specifically and definitely to answer immediately. He always answers that type of prayer immediately. "For every one who asks receives" (Luke 11:10).

The apostle is saying in our text that we must take this matter of prayer seriously and learn what God has promised. In other words, master this subject as you would master any other course of study you undertake. Scientists have mastered various areas in the realm of science. Teachers have become proficient at the art of teaching. Artisans give time and study to their trade. In the same way, we must learn to master the art of praying. For though prayer is the simplest thing in the world—a conversation with God—it also can become the very deepest and most profound experience in your life. As you grow in this matter of praying, you will discover that God is very serious about prayer and that through it he makes his omnipotence and omniscience available to us in terms of specific promises.

When you learn to pray on that basis, you will discover that exciting and unexpected things are constantly happening, that there is a quiet but mighty power at work on which you can rely. And as you learn to pray in this way, you find that a tremendous weapon, a mighty power to influence your own life and the lives of others, is put at your disposal.

OPEN THEIR EYES, LORD

But we are not alone in this battle—this conflict with doubt, dismay, fear, confusion, and uncertainty. No, there are others around us who are weaker and younger in Christ than we are, and there are still others who are stronger than we. But all of us are fighting this battle together. We cannot put on the armor of God for another person, but we can pray for that other person. We can call in reinforcements when we find him engaged in a struggle greater than he can handle for the moment, or perhaps for which he is not fully equipped. It may be, you see, that he has not yet learned how to handle his armor adequately. We are to be aware of other people's problems and pray for them. We are to pray that their eyes will be open to danger, and we are to help them realize how much is available in the armor God has given them, for it is a means of specific help and strength for a specific trial.

Notice how Paul asks this for himself in this very passage. "[Pray] for me, that utterance may be given me in opening my mouth boldly to proclaim the mystery of the gospel" (Ephesians 6:19). This mighty apostle has a deep sense of his need for prayer. He says, "Pray that God may grant to me boldness that I will be so confident of the truth of which I speak that no fear of man will ever dissuade me or turn me aside." You find another notable example of Paul's desire for prayer in the closing verses of the fifteenth chapter of Romans where he asks the Christians to pray for three things specifically: physical safety when he visits Jerusalem; a sensitive, tactful spirit when he speaks to Christians there; and an ultimate opportunity to visit the city of Rome (Romans

15:30–32). Three specific requests, and the record of Scripture is that everyone of them was answered exactly as Paul had asked.

In reading through the prayers of Paul, I find that he deals with many matters. He prays repeatedly for other Christians that their spiritual understanding might be enlightened. He asks that the eyes of their mind—their intelligence—might be opened and unveiled. This repetition in the apostle's prayers indicates the importance of intelligently understanding life—what is true and what is false, what is real and what is phony. It also illustrates the power of the devil to blind and confuse us and to make things look very different from the way they really are. So the repeated prayer of the apostle is, Lord, open their eyes that their understanding may be enlightened, that their intelligence may be clarified, that they may see things as they are.

In the letter of James, the importance of praying for others is forcefully underlined. "My brethren, if any one among you wanders from the truth and some one brings him back, let him know that whoever brings back a sinner from the error of his way will save his soul from death and will cover a multitude of sins" (James 5:19–20).

The prayer of another person can change the whole atmosphere of one person's life, oftentimes overnight. One Christmas eve my family and I were in the Sierra Nevada mountains at Twain Harte. When the sun went down, the landscape around us was dry and barren. A few brown leaves swirled down from the trees; it was a typically bleak winter landscape. But when we awoke the next morning it was to a wonderland of beauty. Every harsh line was softened, every blot was covered. Five inches of snow had fallen during the night and the whole landscape was quietly and marvelously transformed into a fairyland of delight.

I have seen this same thing happen in the life of an individual whose attitude toward the things of God and of reality was hard, stubborn, determined to have his own way. By virtue of prayer, secretly performed in the closet, that person's heart was softened, melted, mellowed, and changed. His total outlook was changed overnight.

Now it does not always happen overnight. Sometimes it takes much longer. Time is a factor which God alone controls, and he never puts a time limit on his instruction concerning prayers. But he constantly calls us to this ministry of prayer both for ourselves and for one another. When we learn to pray as God teaches us to pray, we release in our own lives and in the lives of others the immense resources of God to strengthen the spirit and to give inner stability and power to meet the pressures and problems of life.

Our Father, we know so little about this mighty ministry of prayer. We pray that you will teach us to pray. Forgive us for the way we have often looked at prayer as though it were unimportant, insignificant, an optional thing in our lives. Help us to take it seriously. Help us to realize that you have made this the point of contact between us and you. We pray, then, as the disciples prayed, "Lord teach us to pray." In thy name, amen.

ACKNOWLEDGEMENTS

"The Good Side of the Bad News" originally published as "Exposing the Dark Side" in *Growing Deep in the Christian Life* by Charles Swindoll. © 1986, 1995 by Charles R. Swindoll, Inc. Used by permission of Zondervan Publishing House.

"Sowing Perversion, Deception and Discord" originally published as "Spiritual Deception" in *Storm Warning* by Billy Graham. © 1992 by Billy Graham. Word Publishing, Nashville, Tennessee. Used by permission. All rights reserved.

"Who Won the Showdown in the Desert?" originally published as "Temptation" in *Surprise Endings* by Ron Mehl. © 1993 by Ron Mehl. Multnomah Publishers, Inc. Used by permission.

"The Battle between the Kingdoms" originally published as "The Cross and the Crown" in *Kingdoms in Conflict* by Charles W. Colson. © 1987 by Charles W. Colson. Used by permission of William Morrow & Company.

"The Serpent is Doomed" originally published as "The Serpent is Crushed" in *The Serpent of Paradise* by Erwin W. Lutzer. © 1996 by Erwin W. Lutzer. Moody Bible Institute of Chicago. Moody Press. Used by permission.

"How Satan Causes You to Sin" originally published as "Sin Is Worse Than Satan" in *Future Grace* by John Piper. © 1995 by John Piper. Multnomah Publishers, Inc. Used by permission.

"Don't Listen to Your Loins" taken from *Counterattack* by Jay Carty. © 1988 by Yes Ministries. Used by permission.

"New Age or Old Lie?" originally published as "A New Age?" in *New Age or Old Lie?* by Kerry D. McRoberts. © 1989 by Hendrickson Publishers, Inc. Used by permission. All rights reserved.

NOTES

The Good Side of the Bad News

1. Mark Twain, *Familiar Quotations,* ed. John Bartlett (Boston: Little, Brown & Co., 1955), p. 679.

2. Michael de Montaigne, *Quote Unquote,* ed. Lloyd Cory (Wheaton, Ill.: Victor Books, 1977), p. 297.

3. J. Dwight Pentecost, *Things Which Become Sound Doctrine* (Westwood, N.J.: Fleming H. Revell Co., 1965), pp. 17–18.

4. John R. W. Stott, *Involvement,* vol. 1: *Being a Responsible Christian in a Non-Christian Society* (Old Tappan, N.J.: Fleming H. Revell Co., 1985), pp. 64–65.

5. Charlotte Elliott, "Just As I Am."

6. Catherine Marshall, *A Man Called Peter* (New York: McGraw-Hill, 1951), p. 319.

The Battle between the Kingdoms

1. Acts 17:6–7, NIV.

2. In the second half of the second century, Christians were systematically persecuted. This account of a massacre in the Rhone Valley is not atypical: "Many Christians were tortured in the stocks or in cells. Sanctus, a deacon from Vienna, had red-hot plates applied to his testicles—his poor body was one whole wound and bruise having lost the outward form of a man. Christians who were Roman citizens were beheaded. Others were forced through a gauntlet of whips into the amphitheater and then—given to the beasts. Severed heads and limbs of Christians were displayed, guarded for six days, then burned, the ashes being thrown into the Rhone. One lady, Blandina, was the worst treated of all, tortured from dawn until evening till her torturers were exhausted and marveled that the breath was still in her body. She was then scourged, roasted in the frying pan and finally put in the basket to be tossed to death by wild bulls." Paul Johnson, *History of Christianity* (New York: Atheneum, 1979), 72–73.

Many Christians went to their death praising their King, and such martyrdom became the church's most potent witness. Pagan Romans were convinced that Christ had taken away their pains. As has often been said, the church was built on the martyrs' blood.

3. Historians have questioned Constantine's motives. Some believe it was an effort to save a dying empire, though one contemporary historian has come to a different conclusion. Christianity was practiced only by a small minority. Its universality, the message of Christ Himself, the reliability of written revelation as opposed to myths, began to attract pagan masses. Robin Lane Fox, *Pagans and Christians* (New York: Knopf, 1986).

4. F. F. Bruce, *The Spreading Flame: The Rise and Progress of Christianity from Its First Beginnings to the Coversion of the English* (Grand Rapids, Mich.: Eerdmans, 1958), 293.

5. Etienne Gilson's "Foreword," quoting Fustel de Coulanges, in St. Augustine, *The City of God* (New York: Image/Doubleday, 1958), 15.

6. Alexis de Tocqueville, *The Old Regime and the French Revolution*, translated by Stuart Gilbert (Garden City: Doubleday/Anchor Books, 1955), 149.

7. Ibid., 149.

8. Romans 13:7, NIV.

9. Edmund Clowney, "The Politics of the Kingdom," *Westminster Theological Journal* (Spring 1979), 306.

10. Harold J. Berman, "Atheism and Christianity in the Soviet Union," in *Freedom and Faith: The Impact of Law on Religious Liberty*, ed. Lynn R. Buzzard (Westchester, Ill.: Crossway Books, 1982), 127–43.

11. Oscar Cullman has written, "According to the Jewish, as to the early Christian outlook, the totalitarian state is precisely the classic form of the Devil's manifestation on earth." Oscar Cullman, *The State in the New Testament* (New York: Scribner's, 1956), 74.

12. James Schall reminds us that "if there is any constant temptation of the history of Christianity, from reaction to Christ's rejection of Jewish zealotism on to current debates about the relation of marxism to the Kingdom of God, it is the pressure to make religion a formula for refashioning political and economic structures." James Schall, "The Altar As the Throne," *Churches on the Wrong Road* (Chicago: Regnery/Gateway, 1986), 227.

13. William Blake, "And Did Those Feet," *The Norton Anthology of Poetry*, 3d ed. (New York: W. W. Norton, 1983), 266.

The problem is, as historian Christopher Dawson observed, "There are quite a number of different Jerusalems... There is the Muscovite Jerusalem which has no temple, there is Herr Hitler's Jerusalem which has no Jews, and there is the Jerusalem of the social reformers which is all suburbs. But none of these are Blake's Jerusalem, still less [the kingdom of God]." Christopher Dawson, "Religion and Politics," *Catholicism in Crisis* (June 1985), 8.

All these New Jerusalems are earthly cities established by the will and power of man. And if we believe that the Kingdom of Heaven can be established by political or economic measures, then we can hardly object to the claims of such a state to embrace the whole of life and to demand the total submission of the individual will and conscience.

14. Richard John Neuhaus, *The Naked Public Square* (Grand Rapids, Mich.: Eerdmans, 1984), 231.

15. Patricia Hynds, a Maryknoll lay missionary, was quoted in an article by Juan Tamayo, *Miami Herald* (6 March 1983).

16. Oscar Cullman, *The State in the New Testament* (New York: Scribner's, 1956), 90–91.

Cullman amplifies his point: "The church's task with regard to the state which is posed for all time is thus clear. First, it must loyally give the state everything necessary to its existence. It has to oppose anarchy and all zealotism within its own ranks. Second, it has to fulfill the office of watchmen over the state. That means it must remain in principle critical towards every state and be ready to warn it against transgression of its legitimate limits. Third, it must deny to the state which exceeds its limits, whatever such a state demands that lies within the province of religio-ideological excess; and in its preaching, the church must courageously describe this excess as opposition to God."

17. Hugh T. Kerr, ed., *Compendium of Luther's Theology* (Philadelphia: Westminster Press, 1966), 218.

18. Carl F. H. Henry, "The Gospel for the Rest of Our Century," *Christianity Today* (17 January 1986), 25.

19. Some Christian traditions similarly believe that they can best

model Kingdom values not by involvement in politics but by the establishment of alternative communities in which they live out the teachings
of the Kingdom. In its proper form, this is not a withdrawal from the
world or abandonment of Christian responsibility; nor is it a privatiza-
tion of Christian values as with those who profess to believe but live as
if they do not. It is instead a different strategy to the same end of pro-
viding a witness in the kingdoms of man of the values of the Kingdom
of God. While I do not agree with the generally negative view of government held by such groups, I respect the faithfulness by which they
live their convictions.

20. Quoted in Neuhaus, *The Naked Public Square*, 61.

21. The comment of Baptist minister Isaac Backus is representative:
"Nothing can be a true religion but a voluntary obedience unto his
revealed will, of which each rational soul has an equal right to judge for
himself, every person has an unalienable right to act in all religious
affairs according to the full persuasion of his own mind." "A Declaration
of the Rights of the Inhabitants of the State of Massachusetts-Bay in New
England," in Edwin S. Gaustad, ed., *A Documentary History of Religion in
America, Vol. 1* (Grand Rapids, Mich.: Eerdmans, 1982), 268.

22. One phrase in James Madison's "Memorial and Remonstrance,"
presented to the Commonwealth of Virginia in 1785, succinctly sums
up the thinking of our Founding Fathers: "that Religion or the duty
which we owe to our Creator and the manner of discharging it, can be
directed only by reason and conviction, not by force or violence. The
Religion then of every man must be left to the conviction and conscience of every man; and it is the right of every man to exercise it as
these may dictate." "James Madison's Memorial and Remonstrance,
1785," Edwin S. Gaustad, ed., *A Documentary History of Religion in America:* Vol. I (Grand Rapids, Mich.: Eerdmans, 1982), 262–63.

23. Ibid., 262–263.

24. The concept of a "wall of separation," a phrase incidentally first
used by Jefferson fifteen years after the Constitution was adopted, applied
to institutions of church and state, not religious and political values.

25. Quoted in A. James Reichley, *Religion in American Public Life*
(Washington, D.C.: The Brookings Institute, 1985), 105.

26. Ibid., 360.

The Serpent Is Doomed

1. Frederick S. Leahy, *Satan Cast Out* (Carlisle, Pa.: Banner of Truth, 1975), p. 30.

How Satan Causes You to Sin

1. John Sailhamer, *The Pentateuch as Narrative* (Grand Rapids: Zondervan Publishing House, 1992), pp. 103–4.

Don't Listen to Your Loins

1. This story comes from a newspaper account from several years ago. I was unable to locate the original source.

New Age or Old Lie

1. Matthew Ralston, "She's Having the Time of Her Lives," *People Weekly*, 26 January 1987, p. 31.

2. Ibid., p. 30.

3. Elliot Miller, "The New Age Movement—What Is It?" *People Weekly*, 26 January 1987, p. 31.

4. Ibid., p. 20.

5. Norman Geisler, *Christian Apologetics* (Grand Rapids: Baker, 1976), p. 248.

6. David Spangler, *Revelation: The Birth of a New Age* (Middletown: Lorian, 1976), p. 195.

7. Maureen Orth, "The Sunshine Boy," *Newsweek*, 20 December 1976.

8. Brooks Alexander, "The Rise of Cosmic Humanism: What Is Religion?" *SCP Journal*, Winter 1981–82, p. 3.

9. Ibid.

10. Francis A. Schaeffer and C. Everett Koop, *Whatever Happened to the Human Race?* (Old Tappan: Fleming H. Revell, 1979), p. 148.

11. Marilyn Ferguson, *The Aquarian Conspiracy* (Los Angeles: J. P. Tarcher, Inc., 1980), p. 371.

12. James Sire, *The Universe Next Door* (Downers Grove: InterVarsity Press, 1976), p. 172.

13. Spangler, *Revelation: The Birth of a New Age,* p. 211.

14. Ibid., p. 191.

15. Ralston, "She's Having the Time of Her Lives," p. 33.

16. John Lilly, *The Center of the Cyclone: An Autobiography of Inner Space* (New York: Julian Press, 1972), p. 210.

17. George B. Leonard, "Aikido and the Mind of the West," *Intellectual Digest,* June 1973, p. 20.

18. Ralston, "She's Having the Time of Her Lives," p. 33.

19. Ibid.

20. Katherine Lowry, "Channelers," *Omni,* October 1987, p. 148.

21. Mark Vaz, "Psychic! The Many Faces of Kevin Ryerson" (interview), *Yoga Journal,* July/Aug. 1986, p. 28. Quoted in Elliot Miller, "Channeling Spiritistic Revelations for the New Age," *Christian Research Journal,* Fall 1987, p. 13.

22. Quoted by Tom Minnery, "Unplugging the New Age," *Focus on the Family,* August 1987, p. 3.

23. Reincarnation should not be confused with transmigration. Transmigration is the belief that the soul can return to inhabit any number of things in existence including animals, rocks, trees, etc. Reincarnation is considerably more acceptable to the Western mind.

24. Ralston, "She's Having the Time of Her Lives," p. 32.

25. Benjamin Creme, *The Reappearance of the Christ and the Masters of Wisdom* (Hollywood: Tara Center, Updated pamphlet).

26. *Eerdmans' Handbook to the World Religions* (Grand Rapids: Eerdmans, 1982), p. 31.

27. Mircea Eliade, *The Sacred and the Profane,* trans. William R. Trask (New York: Harper & Row, 1952), pp. 122–23.

28. See Josh McDowell and John Gilchrist, *The Islam Debate* (San Bernardino: Here's Life Publishers, Inc. 1983), for insight into the many inconsistencies within Islam relative to truth claims.

29. Adapted from Harold O. J. Brown, *Heresies* (Garden City, N.Y.: Doubleday, 1984), p. 15.

30. See Josh McDowell, *Evidence That Demands a Verdict* (San

Bernardino: Here's Life Publishers, Inc., 1979), chapter 9, "The Messianic Prophecies of the Old Testament Fulfilled in Christ," pp.141–76. In this chapter, McDowell documents some 332 distinct prophecies literally fulfilled in Jesus of Nazareth.

31. John Warwich Montgomery, *The Shape of the Past* (Ann Arbor: Edwards Brothers, 1962), p. 140.

32. Spangler, *Revelation: The Birth of a New Age*, p. 121.

33. Mark and Elizabeth Clare Prophet, *Climbing the Highest Mountain* (Los Angeles: Summit Lighthouse, 1975), p. xxvi.

34. Creme, *The Reappearance of the Christ and the Masters of Wisdom*, p. 120.

35. Ibid., p. 25.

36. Shirley MacLaine, *Out on a Limb* (New York: Bantam Books, 1983), p. 91.

37. Levi Dowling, *The Aquarian Gospel of Jesus the Christ* (Marina del Rey: De Vorss & Co., 1964), p. 255.

38. Ibid., p. 261.

39. Dharma is a Buddhist doctrine. Dharma refers both to the moral and physical laws governing the universe and to the individual parts of the universe. The universe and everything in it are perceived as originating through the working together of the separate components in existence known as "dharmas." The human being only appears to be an individual; in reality, this is an illusion. The person is rather a part of flowing, continually changing dharmas, which following death rearranges itself to form a new individual.

40. Ferguson, *The Aquarian Conspiracy*, p. 100.

41. Ibid, p. 164.

42. Jessica Lipnack and Jeffrey Stamps, *Networking* (Garden City: Doubleday, 1982), p. 7.

43. Teilhard de Chardin, *The Phenomenon of Man* (New York: Harper & Row, 1961), p. 3.

44. Ferguson, *The Aquarian Conspiracy*, p. 217.

45. Ibid., pp. 62–63.

46. Ibid., p. 25.

47. Ibid., p. 157.

48. Fritjof Capra, *The Turning Point* (Toronto: Bantam Books, 1982), p. 22.

49. Ferguson, *The Aquarian Conspiracy,* p. 28.

50. These lines are from the musical *Hair.*